DANGEROUS GROUNDS

DANGEROUS GROUNDS

Antiwar Coffeehouses and
Military Dissent in the
Vietnam Era

DAVID L. PARSONS

THE UNIVERSITY OF NORTH CAROLINA PRESS

Chapel Hill

This book was published with the assistance of the Authors
Fund of the University of North Carolina Press.

© 2017 The University of North Carolina Press

All rights reserved

The University of North Carolina Press has been a member
of the Green Press Initiative since 2003.

Cover illustration: Soldiers and civilians at the nation's first GI coffeehouse,
the UFO in Columbia, S.C., 1968. Courtesy of Lucy Rutledge.

Library of Congress Cataloging-in-Publication Data
Names: Parsons, David L.
Title: Dangerous grounds : antiwar coffeehouses and military dissent in the
Vietnam era / David L. Parsons.
Description: Chapel Hill : The University of North Carolina Press, [2017] |
Includes bibliographical references and index.
Identifiers: LCCN 2016025852| ISBN 9781469632018 (cloth : alk. paper) |
ISBN 9781469661551 (pbk. : alk. paper) | ISBN 9781469632025 (ebook)
Subjects: LCSH: Vietnam War, 1961–1975—Protest movements—United States. |
Coffeehouses—History—20th century. | United States—History,
Military—20th century. | Soldiers—United States—History—20th century.
Classification: LCC DS559.62.U6 P37 2017 | DDC 959.704/31—dc23
LC record available at https://lccn.loc.gov/2016025852

FOR CLAUDIA

Contents

Acknowledgments ix

GI Coffeehouse Locations, 1968–1974 xi

Introduction 1

1 Setting Up Shop: Coffeehouses Land in America's Army Towns 15

2 Getting Together: Political Activism at GI Coffeehouses 41

3 Repression, Harassment, Intimidation: Crushing the Coffeehouses 65

4 Moving On: A Changing War, a Changing Army, and a Changing Movement 88

Epilogue: Support Our Troops 121

Notes 125

Bibliography 143

Index 155

Acknowledgments

While researching the history of GI coffeehouses, I benefited tremendously from the intellectual and historical perspectives shared generously by several scholars. I'm particularly grateful to Professor Joshua Brown, whose work first awakened me to the possibilities of social and cultural history. My subsequent years working with Professor Brown at the New Media Lab and American Social History Project at the City University of New York Graduate Center continued to broaden my ideas about history, and our conversations always provided me with advice and inspiration that added rigor and passion to my work. Professors Clarence Taylor, Stephen Brier, Gerald Markowitz, and Joshua Freeman also shared critical insights throughout my years at the Graduate Center, without which this book would not have been possible.

I would also like to thank several figures from the coffeehouse movement who were kind enough to share their experiences with me. Barbara Garson, Josh Gould, Howard Levy, and Stephanie Coontz were all generous with their time and patient with my many questions. David Zeiger, a filmmaker and dedicated historian of the GI movement, shared his impressive collection of underground newspapers and related ephemera, located on the website for his film *Sir! No Sir!*, a collection that became one of the foundational sources for my investigation. Most of all, I would like to thank Fred Gardner, the creator of the GI coffeehouse concept, for sharing his time and garage full of primary sources with me. His friendly participation and unique perspective was enormously helpful for this project.

Several colleagues, friends, and family members provided endless enthusiasm and support for my project over the years. In particular, my frequent conversations with Claudia Moreno Parsons and Justin Rogers-Cooper regularly challenged my assumptions and brought fresh viewpoints. And I want to thank my parents, Jim and Linda Parsons, for their unconditional support and belief in me throughout my years of education.

Finally, I'm eternally indebted to my wife, Claudia, whose motivation, inspiration, and love helped me immeasurably in writing this history.

GI Coffeehouse Locations, 1968-1974

Chicago Area Military Project (Chicago, Illinois)
Covered Wagon (Mountain Home, Idaho)
Echo Mike (Los Angeles, California)
Fellowship of the Ring Coffeehouse (Fairbanks, Alaska)
First Amendment Coffeehouse (Frankfurt, Germany)
Fort Dix Coffeehouse (Wrightstown, New Jersey)
Fort Jackson GI Center (Columbia, South Carolina)
Fort Knox Coffeehouse (Muldraugh, Kentucky)
FTA Project (Louisville, Kentucky)
Green Machine (San Diego, California)
Haymarket Square Coffeehouse (Fayetteville, North Carolina)
Hobbit Coffeehouse (Iwakuni, Japan)
Homefront (Colorado Springs, Colorado)
Left Flank (Milwaukee, Wisconsin)
Liberated Barracks GI Project (Kailua, Hawaii)
Oleo Strut (Killeen, Texas)
Pentagon GI Coffeehouse (Oakland, California)
People's Place (Chicago, Illinois)
Potemkin Bookshop (Newport, Rhode Island)
Shelter Half (Tacoma, Washington)
UFO (Columbia, South Carolina)

DANGEROUS GROUNDS

Introduction

Although more than forty years have passed since its official end, the Vietnam War continues to occupy a prominent place in the collective American psyche. The word "Vietnam" exists as a kind of shorthand, regularly invoked to stand in for a whole range of lessons, moral platitudes, and political opinions. Despite its dominant place in public discourse, though, the *meaning* of the Vietnam War remains fundamentally unsettled, its legacy unclear, its lessons and politics as divisive as ever. Decades of public revisionism and Hollywood mythmaking have helped create a series of enduring misconceptions about the era's history.

One particularly misunderstood subject is the movement against the war. Major histories of the antiwar movement, along with popular movies and television programs, have focused most of their attention on the rise and fall of the New Left on college campuses. The typical stars of this story are the idealistic young radicals of organizations like Students for a Democratic Society, one of the leading campus antiwar groups of the era. In the war's early years, Students for a Democratic Society and similar organizations staged some of the nation's first major peace demonstrations on college campuses around the country. The student movement's historic significance is undeniable, but its disproportionate place in public memory obscures the wider history of antiwar activism in the Vietnam era. In reality, of course, antiwar sentiment was not limited to Students for a Democratic Society and other campus groups. Especially in the war's later years, as a majority of Americans came to oppose the war, the antiwar movement grew to include a diverse range of activists and organizations quite distinct from the student movement. For a number of reasons, however, the campus radical persists as the dominant cultural image of Vietnam-era antiwar activism.[1]

A related and equally persistent mythology about the antiwar movement concerns its relationship to American soldiers. Aided by the distortions of conservative politicians from Ronald Reagan to George H. W. Bush to Sarah Palin, along with their supporters and enablers in the news media, the image of angry protesters disrespecting American soldiers has become firmly lodged in American culture. Popular movies like *First Blood* (the first in the Rambo series), *Hamburger Hill, Forrest Gump,* and many others feature patriotic GIs pitted against vindictive and ungrateful antiwar activists. These words and images, repeated endlessly, have produced one of the war's most enduring cultural legends: that antiwar protesters regularly spit on and antagonized uniformed soldiers upon their return from service in Vietnam. The image has become a critical element in a revisionist narrative of the war, invoked in public discourse as proof that the antiwar movement's divisive behavior demoralized our soldiers and helped lose the war. The "spitting story" and related myths trade on false stereotypes of both activists and soldiers, and their continued cultural currency clouds our understanding of the interaction between antiwar politics and the U.S. military.[2]

This book challenges these misconceptions by presenting a more detailed picture of the relationship between the civilian antiwar movement and American soldiers during the Vietnam years. The book's central focus is a network of GI coffeehouses that opened outside a number of American military bases around the country between 1968 and 1974. The GI coffeehouse network was funded and operated by a wide range of organizations and individuals—both inside and outside the American military—who opened more than twenty different antiwar coffeehouse projects throughout the Vietnam War era. Beyond creating comfortable, counterculture-themed hangouts for GIs, the coffeehouses served as resource centers and organizational bases for the growing movement of active-duty soldiers organizing against the war.

The GI movement, as it came to be known, evolved out of a series of isolated acts of resistance in the early years of the war. In 1966, three U.S. Army soldiers—Private First Class James Johnson, Private David Samas, and Private Dennis Mora—were branded the "Fort Hood Three" when they refused to deploy to Vietnam, releasing a joint statement that explained, "We will not be a part of this unjust, immoral, and illegal war."[3] They faced three years of hard labor for their actions. That same year, decorated Green Beret Donald Duncan resigned from the army and became an outspoken public critic of the war, his photo appearing on the February 1966 cover of leading New Left magazine *Ramparts* along with the headline "The Whole Thing Was a Lie!" In 1967, Dr. Howard Levy, a military dermatologist, was court-martialed for his refusal to provide medical training to Special Forces troops bound for Vietnam. Many of the GIs who supported Levy referred to themselves as part of a movement called "RITA" (Resistance inside the Army), scrawling the letters on the walls of barracks, inside their lockers, and on bathroom mirrors. Outside the army, many activists in the antiwar movement revered figures like Levy and Duncan and welcomed the rising GI movement as further evidence of the war's poisonous impact on American life.

Fred Gardner, a San Francisco–based activist and journalist, wrote a number of stories about the nascent GI movement. He became convinced that civilian antiwar activists should find a way to support the men and women resisting the war from inside the armed forces. Gardner recognized that the potential for a mass movement was particularly ripe in the U.S. Army, where nearly 95 percent of all Vietnam-era draftees were sent. To Gardner, this massive pool of young men was a natural breeding ground for antipathy toward the war and military service in general. Indeed, the army had been the first military branch to begin feeling the effects of war fatigue within the ranks, experiencing a dramatic rise in rates of AWOLs, desertions, general insubordination, and drug abuse as early as 1967.[4] The army was also the site of the earliest direct political actions by soldiers in opposition to the war. The Fort Hood Three, the Howard Levy case, and many other high-profile acts of resistance all emerged from the army. If the civilian antiwar movement was looking to connect with a population of demoralized, alienated soldiers, Gardner reasoned, the army was clearly the most likely place to find it. But how could antiwar civilians connect with young GIs stationed at army posts around the country?

A counterculture-themed coffeehouse, thought Gardner, could provide young GIs with access to antiwar literature, a supportive and informed activist staff, and a relaxing space away from military authorities. Such coffeehouses would be serious political projects but would come across mainly as comfortable, hip environments that featured live music, poetry readings, rock posters, and other accoutrements of 1960s youth counterculture. Gardner envisioned a national network of such coffeehouses, buzzing with antiwar conversations and energy, working to support and build a powerful movement of antiwar GIs. In January 1968, he opened the first GI coffeehouse, the UFO in Columbia, South Carolina, outside the army's Fort Jackson.

After the UFO's early success, the GI coffeehouse idea caught on within the civilian antiwar movement. Later that year a series of national antiwar organizations launched a "Summer of Support" to raise money and gain attention for a whole network of coffeehouses based on Gardner's UFO. Within a few years, a large number of different GI coffeehouse projects opened and operated in military towns around the United States (and a few in Japan, Germany, and other global U.S. military outposts). Most of these projects were short-lived, but a small network of flagship coffeehouses, located outside some of the army's most active domestic installations, remained open for several years and contributed to some of the GI movement's most significant actions.

GI coffeehouses, and the GI movement they supported, existed within the context of the wider social, cultural, and political turmoil of the 1960s and 1970s. The era's complicated racial politics are a particularly critical element of this story. Coffeehouses were part of a wave of increased attention and action, driven by the civil rights and black liberation movements, aimed at the army's serious racial issues. Black GIs faced discrimination in nearly every aspect of their army experience, from unequal promotion opportunities, to unfair housing practices, to the army justice system's disproportionate sentencing and harsh jail treatment.[5] Even the war itself was fought unequally. Between 1965 and 1969, blacks made up 14.9 percent of all combat deaths in Vietnam, well above their representation in the wider population.[6] These and other issues helped fuel widespread and diverse acts of resistance on the part of black GIs. Evasion and desertion rates among black soldiers rose dramatically after 1968, as did other acts of protest and disobedience. Reflecting the wider black movement's rising militancy, a significant number of black GIs were deeply resentful of the Vietnam War and the American military. In the later years of the war, black soldiers had gained such a reputation for insubordination and resistance that, in many units, they were considered unreliable on the front lines of combat.[7]

Organizers at GI coffeehouses found that race was often the driving element of GI activism on post. In one of the coffeehouse network's first political actions, civilian peace activists provided legal and media support for a group of black soldiers at Fort Hood who refused to deploy to Chicago to serve as riot control at the August 1968 Democratic National Convention. Along with many others, the "Fort Hood 43" case displays the intersection of antiwar and racial politics that characterized much of the coffeehouse network's history. As coffeehouses became more deeply involved in the politics of the GI movement, navigating the era's sharp racial divisions was a significant part of their development.

Widespread changes in the social, political, and economic status of women in American society also made a significant impact on the direction of coffeehouse activism.[8] Coffeehouse organizers often employed the language of women's liberation to articulate their antiwar positions. GI coffeehouses were often characterized as "liberated sexual territory" where soldiers could escape the narrowly proscribed gender roles they were expected to fill on post. GI coffeehouses and GI underground newspapers promoted a specifically antimilitary version of women's liberation, reflecting a prominent feeling among antiwar activists that sexism, along with racism and imperialism, was a key element in the military's weapons of oppression. When a GI coffeehouse near Fort Dix, New Jersey, organized an antiwar parade in 1971, for example, participants issued a list of demands meant to summarize the GI movement's central complaints. "End reinforcement of unnatural and oppressive sexual roles" was third on the list.[9]

Most coffeehouse projects made a conscious effort to reach out to local military women. At the time, women in the military could be divided into two major groups: active-duty women (those actually enlisted in the military) and military dependents (wives of enlisted men). Each group had a particular set of problems and needs, and in developing strategies that addressed those needs, coffeehouse organizers became one of the first major voices calling public attention to the unique position of women in relation to the army. GI organizers based in Fayetteville, for example, initiated the Fort Bragg Women's Project at the Haymarket Square Coffeehouse in 1971. The project sought to organize local army wives into a political collective, reasoning that women could play a powerful role in a movement to transform military culture: "We felt strongly that our main emphasis in Fayetteville should be GI wives. It is our opinion that the GI movement is the only mass working class movement at this time; their [GIs'] awareness comes from their close relationship with imperialism. Wives are similarly touched except that they don't literally go to Nam themselves. Because of the Army's blatant sexism regarding 'dependents' and its overt objectification of women, we do feel that most women in an Army town are a potential force against the Army."[10] Through coffeehouse women's groups, the relentless satire of military machismo featured in GI newspapers, and various efforts at off-post consciousness-raising, a strong current of 1970s feminism runs throughout the coffeehouse network's history.[11]

Labor politics was also a significant force within the GI movement and shaped the direction of political activity at GI coffeehouses. The GI movement's working-class character was in part a product of the war's disproportionate impact on the country's working class and poor, who served at far higher rates than men from middle- and upper-class backgrounds. The GIs who protested the war often brought a strident labor radicalism to their political activism. While many GI activists had discovered antiwar politics while serving in the army, many others had been activists prior to their service and joined the armed forces with the express intent of organizing resistance from within. One such soldier was Andy Stapp, who enlisted in 1967 and proceeded to organize a soldier's union called the American Servicemen's Union. His efforts earned him a swift discharge in 1968, but Stapp and the American Servicemen's Union continued to organize soldiers throughout the Vietnam era, and Stapp himself was a regular fixture in GI coffeehouses and at GI movement events. Though it never gained official recognition and dissolved after the war's end, Stapp's union in the 1970s claimed tens of thousands of members, with chapters at nearly every military base around the world.[12] Stapp's radicalism, like that of many activists in the GI movement, drew on principles from labor and other left organizations.

Especially in the coffeehouse network's early stages, civilian organizers tended to come from middle-class backgrounds, most often entering the movement through their college's Students for a Democratic Society chapter. The class differences between activists and GIs were a constant topic of discussion at coffeehouses. As the movement developed, however, these differences lessened considerably, with working-class activists making up a larger portion of civilian coffeehouse staff. Part of the reason for this shift was the involvement of organizations like the Socialist Workers Party and its youth corollary, the Young Socialist Alliance. These Trotskyist organizations sought to channel widespread antiwar sentiment into a full-scale working-class rebellion in the U.S. Army.[13] As part of that effort, the Socialist Workers Party and the Young Socialist Alliance played an active role in the funding and leadership of several coffeehouse projects, changing the class composition of the GI movement's civilian wing in the network's later years. Their involvement was part of several important trends in the larger antiwar movement—including civil rights and black liberation politics, radical feminism, and youth counterculture—that contributed to the GI coffeehouse network's overall energy and direction.

This book focuses on three of the longest lasting and most active coffeehouse projects: the UFO, mentioned above; the Oleo Strut in Killeen, Texas (outside Fort Hood); and the Shelter Half in Tacoma, Washington (outside Fort Lewis). These coffeehouses existed near some of the most important army installations of the Vietnam era; each played a critical part in the operation of the Vietnam War. Over the course of several years, these three coffeehouses evolved into popular local hangouts, centers of political organization, and subjects of significant controversy. The details of their stories provide entry into the complicated intersection of antiwar politics and the U.S. Army during an increasingly unpopular war.

Framed by the stories of these three flagship coffeehouses, the book considers the coffeehouse movement as a whole, tracking the development of many other projects through the entirety of the network's history. The book synthesizes a diverse range of sources, including the GI underground press, records of antiwar organizations, editorials and letters in local newspapers, legal documents, trial transcripts, government records, congressional investigations, and interviews conducted with participants in the coffeehouse movement. The story unfolds chronologically and is divided into four major chapters, each focused on a different phase of the coffeehouse network's history.

Chapter 1 explains the origins of the coffeehouse concept, its founding ethos and organizing principles, and the practical challenges of opening antiwar businesses in often hostile communities. This chapter follows Fred Gardner and a host of other antiwar activists as they established the first coffeehouse projects, their experiences reflecting the often significant regional differences antiwar activists encountered in military towns in the late 1960s. Since each of these towns maintained deep social, political, and economic ties to the American military establishment, coffeehouse organizers came face-to-face with local cultures deeply invested in preserving a military-friendly status quo. Over time they developed a variety of strategies to overcome some of these challenges, with varying degrees of success, particularly after the antiwar movement's so-called Summer of Support in 1968 brought an influx of funds and support staff.

Chapter 2 focuses on the different kinds of political activism organized at GI coffeehouses once they were established in multiple locations through 1968. Coffeehouses became the primary institutional components of a diverse outburst of political activity in the U.S. military, particularly concentrated in the U.S. Army. In Columbia, the UFO coffeehouse provided an instrumental organizational base for GIs involved in the "Fort Jackson Eight" case, which challenged army officials to redefine ideas of free speech for enlisted men. Similarly, at the Oleo Strut in Killeen, Texas, soldiers and civilians initiated a broad-based defense campaign after GI Richard Chase was imprisoned for his refusal to engage in riot control training. In addition, the Oleo Strut supported a GI-led boycott of Tyrrell's Jewelry, a national chain of stores that, according to many GIs, exploited vulnerable and homesick soldiers in order to sell rings and necklaces. At the Shelter Half coffeehouse, activists staged an "Aquatic Invasion of Fort Lewis," a piece of guerrilla theater that kick-started larger demonstrations in and around the massive Tacoma army post. In all of these cases, GI coffeehouses were catalysts for a wide range of tactics and strategies, evolving into dynamic political institutions that addressed a number of important concerns, both war-related and otherwise, felt by soldiers in the Vietnam-era army.

Chapter 3 details what happened when GI coffeehouses caught the attention of post officials, government authorities, local and national politicians, reactionary vigilantes, and others who saw the coffeehouses as a significant threat to a revered national institution. The House Un-American Activities Committee, during its final years of existence, held a series of congressional hearings to investigate alleged communist subversion of the U.S. military. In the first of these hearings, the committee interrogated antiwar movement leaders Rennie Davis and Tom Hayden about their role in the GI coffeehouse network, with several committee members expressing outrage at the very idea of an antiwar coffeehouse designed for military personnel. A later series of congressional hearings in 1971 focused exclusively on the coffeehouse network, collecting data from dozens of coffeehouse projects and publicly accusing coffeehouse organizers of attempting to subvert the American armed forces during a time of war.

These federal investigations were accompanied by a relentless campaign of harassment and intimidation at the local level, with police departments, angry locals, post authorities, and many others combining to create a hostile, often frightening atmosphere for those involved with GI coffeehouse projects. In Muldraugh, Kentucky, for example, the Fort Knox Coffeehouse was firebombed twice before being run out of town by local police, and in Mountain Home, Idaho, a popular coffeehouse project called the Covered Wagon was burned to the ground in 1971. And in some of the most dramatic developments in the coffeehouse network's history, both the Shelter Half and UFO coffeehouses faced serious legal actions that closed the projects and subjected their

Introduction 9

organizers to arrest and imprisonment. Collectively, these attacks crippled the coffeehouse network and bankrupted its limited funds. But perhaps more important, the often severe repression and harassment showed that the coffeehouses had hit a nerve. Government officials and military policy makers, recognizing the seriousness of the crisis that coffeehouses seemed to represent, embarked on a series of efforts to disrupt their operations.

Coffeehouse organizers quickly learned that military towns took their connections to the armed forces very seriously. In Catherine Lutz's *Homefront: A Military City and the American Twentieth Century*, the anthropologist and historian examines Fayetteville, North Carolina (home of the Fort Bragg army post), as a representative military city, showing how mobilization for war can have a totalizing impact on regions that have become virtually dependent on the U.S. military for their economic well-being. According to Lutz, this dependence breeds a kind of ideological homogeneity enforced through local politics, culture, and social relations. Lutz's history includes the story of Quaker House, a GI movement center created by antiwar organizers in 1970. Months after opening, Quaker House was burned to the ground, with several civilians and GIs injured in the blaze; a police investigation concluded it was arson but no one was ever charged for the crime. On the editorial pages of local newspapers, some Fayetteville citizens expressed virulent hostility to the antiwar movement's presence in their city. While this hostility was often expressed in cultural terms ("these doped up, whining, dirty, non-working, non-tax-paying, dutiless [sic] non-Americans should be behind bars where they belong," one letter read), there was an undeniable allegiance to American military values underlying the cultural revulsion.[14] To many citizens of Fayetteville and other similar military-centered American communities, GI coffeehouses and other antiwar projects geared toward American GIs felt like a direct attack on local values, and they lashed out in perceived defense of those values.

Chapter 4 surveys the coffeehouse network's later years, when major shifts in both the operation of the war and in military policy challenged the GI movement to develop new organizing strategies. Beginning in 1969, the Nixon administration altered course in Vietnam, withdrawing ground troops while accelerating U.S. bombing campaigns in the region. As the U.S. Air Force and the U.S. Navy took on a heavier responsibility for fighting the war, the force and direction of military antiwar activism shifted to these other branches. Organizers at the primarily army-oriented GI coffeehouse networks had to adapt their political work to the concerns of a different constituency of military men and women. Their work was also influenced by the momentous changes in recruiting policy and military culture taking place throughout the late 1960s and early 1970s. The federal government was enmeshed in the complicated process of ending the draft system and converting to an "all-volunteer force." This process included a multipost experimental program called VOLAR (Volunteer Army) that attempted to update the experience of army service for a post-Vietnam generation. The VOLAR program, and the larger changes it signaled, had a major impact on the thinking of GI activists and their allies at GI coffeehouses who worked to find programs and ideas that spoke to soldiers in a rapidly changing army.

The antiwar movement was also transforming during this later period. The influence of black nationalism and other forms of identity politics expanded the movement's perspectives and strategies while also leading to serious divisions. These divisions were often visible at GI coffeehouses, where struggles over racial issues came bubbling to the surface throughout the network's later years. Despite these points of tension, however, the antiwar movement's more diverse composition and focus also brought an influx of new energy and ideas. Even as GI and civilian activists argued over political ideology, the GI movement itself reached a peak moment of cultural influence and national attention.

In 1971, antiwar celebrities like Jane Fonda and Donald Sutherland toured the network with an antiwar-themed revue called the "FTA Show" (the initials either stood for "Free the Army" or "Fuck the Army," then common catchphrases in the GI movement). The popular show drew large crowds of GIs, whose numbers and enthusiasm reflected the depth of antiwar sentiment among American service members. The underground GI press also reached a peak of production, publishing thousands of underground newspapers at bases around the world. GI coffeehouses often served as the printing and distribution centers for this extraordinary output of independent media, helping navigate the serious hazards and challenges of producing antiwar literature for active-duty GIs. During this time, the GI press developed an antiauthority aesthetic and ethos that reflected the depth of alienation felt by the soldier rank and file in the Vietnam era.

In this period, coffeehouse organizers held a series of national GI movement conferences, the largest of which took place in Williams Bay, Wisconsin, in 1971. More than 100 GIs, veterans, and civilians spent five days wrestling with the implications of the changing war, the changing conditions of military service, and the changing direction of left politics. Their discussions reflect the different forces at work in the antiwar movement during the post-1968 era. From Third World liberation and Black Power, to drugs and counterculture, to gender and sexuality, GI organizers took on a range of political trends and ideologies in considering the direction of their activism. These years witnessed a subsequent broadening of political activity at GI coffeehouses, including an increased focus on military counseling services, bringing attention to rising problems like post-traumatic stress disorder and veteran unemployment, among many other issues. In the final days of the GI coffeehouse network, the antiwar movement was simultaneously expanding and collapsing under the weight of internal divisions and a changing political landscape.

Although the coffeehouse phenomenon faded out along with most other antiwar projects as the Vietnam War came to an end, over the course of its brief lifetime the coffeehouse network played a critical role in the larger GI movement. For the thousands of active-duty soldiers, veterans, and civilians who participated in antiwar activities during the Vietnam era, coffeehouses were a central element of the experience. They became indispensable to the movement's success, used to organize demonstrations, distribute literature, produce underground newspapers, and hold meetings away from post authorities. The existence of an off-post GI coffeehouse was often a determining factor in the growth and long-term survival of local GI antiwar organizations.

Coffeehouses were the central physical spaces in which the GI movement planned activities, published political literature, and made contact with civilian antiwar activists and organizations. As such, they conferred a degree of legitimacy to the actions of antiwar soldiers, amplifying their voices to the public and establishing them as important components of a multipronged national effort to end the war. In her work on feminist activism in the early 1970s, anthropologist Anne Enke examines the importance of institutional spaces like coffeehouses, bars, and movement centers in giving political feminism a public face and helping American women locate sites of resistance. In her book *Finding the Movement: Sexuality, Contested Space, and Feminist Activism*, Enke asks, "How does one locate a movement that could reach a woman in her home and at the same time seem utterly inaccessible to her? A movement that was 'everywhere' and yet nowhere the same? A movement nearly infinite in its origins as well as its continued and changing expressions?"[15] In answering these questions, Enke asserts the vitality of physical spaces developed by feminist activists, arguing that deliberately politicized spaces gave definition to an amorphous movement.

GI coffeehouses, like the feminist institutions that Enke describes, similarly created a physical reality for a set of political ideals, providing sites for American soldiers to locate a civilian antiwar movement that no doubt seemed inaccessible to GIs stationed at often remote military outposts. As antiwar sentiment increased throughout the army in the later years of the Vietnam War, GI coffeehouses helped give public voice to soldiers with limited opportunities to formulate and articulate political critiques. The GI underground press was particularly important in this regard, with coffeehouses evolving into busy printing presses that sustained a robust stream of antiwar information and opinions delivered directly (often covertly) to active-duty soldiers around the world. In an age of instantly accessible digital information, it is important to recognize that, during the Vietnam War era, access to information was more easily controlled by institutional authorities. Possession of printing technology like mimeograph machines and paper presses played a critical role in allowing alternative political and cultural ideas to find wider audiences.

In his book *Working Class War: American Combat Soldiers and Vietnam*, historian Christian Appy points out that access to "complete or thoughtful criticism of the war" and "alternative political and cultural perspectives" was a central factor in determining a young man's attitude toward military service.[16] According to Appy, this access was much more available to middle-class men more likely to go to college or to have friends and family members in college. Particularly in the later years of the Vietnam War, though, many places outside of college campuses had developed to provide the kinds of access to alternative perspectives for working-class men that, earlier in the war, had largely been confined to college campuses. Churches, the alternative press, philanthropic organizations, and labor unions were often sites of heated debates about the war and related issues. The GI coffeehouse network was an important part of these efforts, creating institutions that offered alternatives to the onslaught of pro-war, patriotic perspectives in the mainstream media and within the military itself.

The history of the GI coffeehouse network complicates the widely misunderstood interplay between antiwar soldiers and the civilian peace movement, upending the stereotype of angry protesters spitting on heroic war veterans. Beyond challenging popular mythology about the war, though, the story also provides unique insight into the internal politics of the antiwar movement and the wider landscape of American politics and society in the late 1960s and early 1970s. GI coffeehouses, and the GI movement in which they played a vital part, show us how and why antiwar organizations began reaching out to

U.S. soldiers in the late 1960s; how army authorities and government officials responded to the interaction of GIs and antiwar civilians; how communities outside military bases maintained and defended their strong economic and cultural ties to the military establishment; how GI antiwar projects faced relentless government surveillance and intimidation; how the era's racial politics shaped both the possibilities and limits of antiwar organizations; how dissent flowed through different branches of the U.S. military as the operation of the war evolved; how the character and concerns of the Left and antiwar movement expanded after 1968; and, most important, how radical civilians, veterans, and active-duty GIs worked together to organize unprecedented dissent within the U.S. Army during one of the most divisive wars in the nation's history. As some of the central sites of this extraordinary resistance, GI coffeehouses have vital stories to tell.

Setting Up Shop

Coffeehouses Land in America's Army Towns

> It's unprecedented in American history that we have a movement within the military that is opposing a war which the United States government is waging. That's unprecedented. And it seems to me that the Army and Navy and the Marines have something to do with power; and there is the possibility that the peace movement can have that power on their side. Therefore, the peace movement ought to be supporting the GI movement.
>
> Dr. Howard Levy, *Los Angeles Free Press*, May 1970

FRED GARDNER'S COFFEEHOUSE CONCEPT

In the summer of 1963, Fred Gardner's path seemed set. He had just graduated from Harvard, where he had been a star undergraduate reporter and editor at the *Harvard Crimson*, writing articles on arts, culture, and politics during the height of the Kennedy years. Among the newspaper's young staff, rumor had it that the Kennedy administration regularly read only three newspapers: the *New York Times*, the *Washington Post*, and the *Harvard Crimson*. Gardner later recalled, "For a brief time, I felt like I had a pipeline directly to the White House."[1] After graduation, he immediately landed a job as an editor at *Scientific American*. As he strode into the magazine's slick Madison Avenue offices that summer, he imagined himself at the beginning of a promising career as a New York City writer.

Despite these personal achievements, Gardner was troubled by the headlines throughout the year, concerned that America's involvement in South Vietnam might lead to a wider war. He was especially worried that he hadn't yet fulfilled his obligation for military service. Since he was no longer enrolled in college, being drafted was suddenly a real possibility. In an effort to minimize the disruption to his life and career, as well as to avoid being shipped overseas, in November 1963 Gardner enlisted as an army reservist. He spent the next six months training at Fort Polk in Leesville, Louisiana, before returning to his writing career. Just as he had hoped, by the summer of 1964 he had gotten his military service "out of the way" and moved on with his life. Over the next few years, he got married, had children, and watched with mounting horror as the Vietnam War spun out of control. "The war drove me completely crazy," he later explained.[2] In 1967 his marriage disintegrated.

After his divorce, at twenty-five years old, Gardner moved to San Francisco for a fresh start. He found himself drawn to the city that stood at the center of a burgeoning cultural and political revolution and eager to become more involved in the growing movement against the war. He was particularly interested in the radical political potential of American soldiers and was frustrated that major New Left organizations did not pay them more attention. By ignoring American soldiers, Gardner thought, the Left was missing an opportunity to connect with a massive number of disaffected young men, particularly in the U.S. Army, where the majority of draftees were serving. He imagined an army of young soldiers who were not particularly excited about serving in the Vietnam-era armed forces: "By 1967 the Army was filling up with people who would rather be making love to the music of Jimi Hendrix than war to the lies of Lyndon Johnson. People were serving because they'd been drafted. Or they 'volunteered' because they'd gotten in trouble with the law, or been told they needed an honorable discharge in order to get a job. Almost everybody went in ambivalent about whether the war was worth it—the risk, the interruption to their lives."[3] If you want to stop the war, Gardner thought, one way might be to reach out to those soldiers, to help build an antiwar movement *within* the army.

Gardner had reason to hope for an uprising among the ranks. As the war in Vietnam escalated in 1965 and 1966, instances of rebellion, insubordination, and other forms of antiwar resistance were on the rise. By 1967, at army posts across the country, individual and group demonstrations were drawing national attention and became known as the GI movement. These acts of resistance took infinite forms throughout the war's duration, ultimately creating a significant crisis for military and government officials.[4] Vietnam veterans were also increasingly speaking out against the war. On April 15, 1967, a group of six veterans participated in the Spring Mobilization, a massive New York City peace demonstration, marching behind a handmade placard carrying a simple, searing slogan: "Vietnam Veterans Against the War." After the march, other veterans joined the original group and formed an official organization bearing the same attention-grabbing name.[5] By the following summer, Vietnam Veterans Against the War chapters were springing up around the country. This organization, along with other instances of GI resistance, captured the imagination of civilian antiwar activists like Fred Gardner, who saw great power in an alliance of soldiers and civilians. The energy and authority that soldiers and veterans were bringing to the antiwar movement was undeniably compelling. But could civilians find a way to help harness that energy?

In Gardner's mind, one key to bridging the gap between the organized Left and American GIs lay in the rise of youth counterculture. In San Francisco, he spent much of his time hanging out at the various counterculture establishments that then lined the streets of the city's North Beach neighborhood, an area teeming with revolutionary cultural and political energy. He drew particular inspiration from the radical coffeehouses that offered something more than the requisite folk music and cappuccinos—the places that had tables full of radical literature, that often hosted political speeches and meetings, and that served as de facto bases of operation for a range of local political organizations. Using the common language of sex, drugs, and rock and roll, these coffeehouses were attempting to build a real countercultural politics.

As Gardner sat in these North Beach coffeehouses throughout the summer of 1967, an idea struck him. He recalled his service at Fort Polk in Leesville, Louisiana, a few years earlier. While spending his off time in dingy dive bars and pool halls, he lamented that there were no local hangouts that reflected the vibrant youth culture embraced by so many soldiers of the era. In 1960s Leesville (which many soldiers referred to as "Diseaseville"), "the only places to hang out . . . were seedy, segregated bars serving watered-down drinks for a dollar a shot, a rip-off."[6] Gardner thought the same was probably true of most army towns around the country. He was sure that a great number of GIs would appreciate a hip place to spend time near their post and wagered that a significant portion of those soldiers might also be opposed to the Vietnam War. As he saw it, a hip antiwar coffeehouse, designed for GIs, might be an effective way of starting conversations between antiwar soldiers and civilians. At the very least, he reasoned, it would provide GIs with a comfortable environment to spend time off-post. In late 1967, he resolved to open such a coffeehouse outside one of the most active army training posts in the country.

Fort Jackson, located outside Columbia, South Carolina, was the site of some of the most significant and visible events of the growing GI movement. One of the U.S. Army's largest training posts, Fort Jackson was home to a great number of the military's youngest recruits. During the Vietnam War, the post had a transient population of roughly 20,000 young men, the majority of whom were either recent draftees or "draft-motivated volunteers" who had joined the army under some duress.[7] As the war became more unpopular, particularly among young people like the thousands stationed at Fort Jackson, the post experienced a sharp increase in cases of dissent and insubordination.

In 1967, the post made national headlines with the trial of Howard Levy, an army doctor who refused his assignment to provide medical training for Special Forces troops headed to Vietnam.[8] Dr. Levy was convicted of disobedience and making disloyal statements about U.S. policy in Vietnam. He was dishonorably discharged and incarcerated in military prison for three years. In antiwar circles, Levy was widely admired for his principled stand against the war.[9] Fred Gardner was one such admirer. As he sat in his San Francisco apartment clipping newspaper articles about Levy's trial, he became convinced that Columbia, South Carolina, would be a perfect site for the first GI coffeehouse.[10]

In the mid-1960s, Columbia was regarded as one of the most military-friendly cities in the country. Over the course of several decades, the presence of military camps and other installations had come to be seen as critical to Columbia's economic health, and the city itself became much more directly concerned with fostering a pro-military culture to encourage further military development in the area.[11] "Camp Jackson," as it was first called, had been established in 1917 as the First World War demanded a dramatic expansion of troop levels and training posts. After the war, however, the population of military personnel who had turned Columbia into a bustling military town (with an attendant explosion of local businesses catering to military needs) declined rapidly, and city leaders began to actively lobby the federal government for a more permanent military presence in Columbia. As World War II accelerated, Fort Jackson was finally converted into a permanent army installation, and in 1968 local officials successfully persuaded the Pentagon to officially annex Fort Jackson into the city proper. It was during the height of the Vietnam War, then, that Columbia's leaders explicitly worked to reinforce the city's total alignment with military goals and values; in both an operational and ideological sense, Columbia and Fort Jackson became a single entity.¹²

A permanent military presence provided the Columbia community with a stable and prosperous economy. Local businesses were booming through the 1940s and 1950s, when hundreds of thousands of military men and women moved to the area, creating a ready-made consumer base. At midcentury, "soldiers, civilians, wives, and sweethearts (real, potential, and alleged) poured into the Midlands. Rents soared, restaurants and beer joints boomed, and, for all practical purposes, the Great Depression became a distant memory."¹³ While there was some controversy among city leaders about the influx of bars, nightclubs, and pool halls bringing a certain brand of moral decline to the area (prostitution increased exponentially, for example), for the most part Columbia's business and political community embraced the city's conversion to one of the nation's largest military towns.

Most military-oriented towns, Columbia included, invariably featured downtown districts lined with small businesses offering cheap thrills to lonely and homesick GIs. To Gardner, these places created a "violent, venal atmosphere . . . ringed by strips of bars, whorehouses, jewelry emporiums, and pawnshops," making for a complacent, demoralized group of soldiers.¹⁴ Of course, Gardner had more in mind than just cultural alternatives: he thought that a counterculture coffeehouse, staffed by young civilian radicals, could provide a gateway to a more concentrated antiwar activism on the part of soldiers themselves: "I figured that people working at the coffeehouses, just by listening to GIs' gripes, taking them seriously and maybe distributing them in leaflet form, would help soldiers see that their problems weren't 'merely' personal but widespread and historical. In time, there would develop a network of organizers in the towns and in the Army itself whom soldiers would consider politically trustworthy—because they had a record of telling the truth about conditions."¹⁵

Reluctant to proselytize directly to active-duty soldiers, Gardner envisioned the role of coffeehouse staff as essentially supporting and nurturing antiwar sentiment among GIs, offering them a safe environment and organizational skills to foster the development of their own political activities. Gardner felt that GIs were under enough pressure as it was and would be unlikely to appreciate a hard sales pitch from an overeager activist. Civilian staff should thus take the lead from GIs, rather than vice versa. The coffeehouses would serve mainly as support institutions for empowering disaffected soldiers to channel their energy into political action.¹⁶

Gardner spent the summer of 1967 sharing his coffeehouse idea with just about anyone who would listen. He found a business partner, a friend named Donna Mickleson, and the two pitched the idea to a few of the more prominent countercultural figures around the Bay Area. One early supporter was Alan Myerson, owner and operator of the Committee, a left-wing improv troupe made up of actors from Second City in Chicago. The Committee's cabaret theater in North Beach had become a center for all kinds of radical performances since opening in an abandoned indoor bocce ball court in 1963. In addition to offering business advice, Myerson shared Gardner's coffeehouse idea with local concert promoter Bill Graham, owner of the Fillmore Theater, who donated dozens of rock and roll posters from his infamous San Francisco venue in support of the project.[17] After failing to convince anyone to take on the responsibility of funding and operating the first GI coffeehouse, Gardner and Mickleson finally decided to open it themselves. Leaving San Francisco and driving to Columbia in the fall of 1967, they thought about the uneasy task that lay before them: to open an explicitly antiwar coffeehouse outside one of the army's most active training centers.

"A SORE SPOT IN OUR CRAW": THE UFO LANDS IN COLUMBIA

Gardner and Mickleson arrived in Columbia in September 1967, aware that they were entering hostile territory. Gardner hid his intentions of turning their rental house into a crash pad for "soldiers and organizers, smoking grass and listening to *Sgt. Pepper's Lonely Hearts Club Band*," by fabricating a cover story that he and Mickleson were a married couple whose children would be arriving soon.[18] The pair then went in search of a venue for their coffeehouse, eventually renting a space at 1732 Main Street, in the center of downtown Columbia. They immediately went to work transforming what had been a tropical-themed "Hawaiian" bar into a counterculture coffeehouse, replacing tiki torches and plastic flamingos with photos of Bob Dylan and Janis Joplin, along with the Bill Graham–donated rock posters.

Mickleson hung a psychedelic hand-painted sign reading "UFO" on the outside of the building, officially opening the coffeehouse for business in January 1968. From a cultural standpoint, the owners made no effort to conceal their hip, sardonic orientation, with the aforementioned posters including one of a cannabis plant and another of President Lyndon Johnson awkwardly holding his pet beagle by its ears.[19] The interior of the UFO was "modestly furnished with wooden tables and folding chairs, an area for a band, and displays of reading material featuring alternative newspapers from around the country, such as the *Berkeley Barb*, *The Village Voice* (New York), *The Great Speckled Bird* (Atlanta), and numerous pamphlets, as well as mainstream newspapers and periodicals."[20] The coffeehouse's location, on Main Street in the heart of downtown Columbia, made it highly visible to the city's leaders. It was directly across the street from Columbia's city hall and, perhaps more important, next door to the Elite Epicurean Restaurant, the city's popular gathering spot for local politicos. As the owner of the Elite put it, "We catered to the establishment, and they were the anti-establishment."[21]

The UFO was almost instantly popular, especially among Columbia's high school and college students. But there were also large numbers of soldiers from Fort Jackson visiting the UFO every week, some of whom were eager to organize political activity on post.[22] During daytime hours the UFO operated as any other coffeehouse, serving the usual coffee, tea, and soft drinks, in addition to fresh fruit and locally baked pastries, in a quiet atmosphere, with most customers reading or chatting in small groups. In the evenings, though, the lights dimmed and rock music played from the UFO's hi-fi sound system (on nights when live rock and folk acts were not onstage). The image of American soldiers hanging out in a psychedelic coffeehouse garnered national attention. Just a few months after the UFO opened, a reporter for the *New York Times* visited the coffeehouse. He noted that the smoky mood and psychedelic decor of the UFO resembled establishments in "Greenwich Village or Chicago's Old Town," notorious enclaves of beat and hippie counterculture in 1960s America. The patrons of the UFO were an odd mix of students and young people wearing "miniskirts, Nehru jackets, and beads" alongside clean-cut GIs from Fort Jackson.[23]

As the UFO gained attention, local authorities expressed their concerns about its impact on their town. An official from the chamber of commerce, Thomas Fitzpatrick, told the *Times* reporter, "The so-called coffeehouse is a sore spot in our craw," capturing the visceral distaste with which many of Columbia's citizens regarded the UFO. Fitzpatrick, like a number of city authorities, was fond of pointing out that Columbia had twice been designated an "All America City" and that the city wished to maintain its reputation.[24] Local police were initially employed to this end (later to be joined by military intelligence officers, the FBI, and other government agencies), making nightly visits to the UFO to search for evidence of drugs, to ticket vehicles, and to generally harass its patrons and staff. Chief of Detectives Harry T. Snipes explained, "We just feel like we don't want it in town. We feel it is a bad influence on our youngsters. There are people with whiskers. Some wear sandals. We check it at least once a night, especially to see if there are drugs or addicts in there." To city police, the UFO seemed to represent the enemy camp in a burgeoning culture war, and they did everything in their power to disrupt its existence.[25]

Local police were just one part of a number of organizations and leaders who saw the UFO coffeehouse as a threat to the town's relationship with Fort Jackson and the U.S. military. South Carolina's political and economic leaders were deeply invested in impressing the military establishment that had bestowed so much on the state since the 1940s. During the post–World War II era, that leadership was made up mainly of Democrats, who controlled a majority of the state's major offices, from governor to senator, and whose close relationship to the U.S. military was centered in Columbia, the state's capital. L. Mendel Rivers, congressman from Charleston, was actively involved in Fort Jackson's affairs as chairman of the House Armed Services Committee. Historian Bruce Schulman credits Rivers in particular for exploiting Columbia's military connections to win massive federal support for the city's further expansion: "Into his district, Rivers ... poured an air force base, a naval base, a Polaris missile maintenance center, a naval shipyard, a submarine training station, a naval hospital, a mine warfare center, and the Sixth Naval District Headquarters. As if that was not enough, defense contractors like McDonnell-Douglas, Avco, GE, and Lockheed established factories in the area. One of the congressman's colleagues joked, 'You put anything else down there in your district, Mendel, it's going to sink.'"[26] Along with Senator J. Strom Thurmond, who had been a two-star general in the Army Reserve and who was widely known for his military connections, Rivers ensured that Columbia's economic fate was powerfully connected to the U.S. military.[27] These men provided a link from the local affairs of Fort Jackson to the upper echelons of the federal government, and their allegiance to the military's strong presence in Columbia made them see the UFO coffeehouse as an affront to both local and national values. Their concerns grew more pronounced when it became clear, in January 1968, that the UFO intended to help organize soldiers at Fort Jackson.

That month, the Tet Offensive had captured the attention of the nation; its scenes of intense urban violence were being broadcast into living rooms, which created a sharp drop in public support for the war. Seizing the moment, GIs at Fort Jackson translated their frustrated conversations at the coffeehouse into the first major organized action against the Vietnam War on an

American military base. The organizers, led by Specialist Martin Blumsack, had received permission from Fort Jackson's post chaplain to use the post's chapel for an "hour of meditation" to express "grave concern" about the war.[28] The pray-in, as it came to be known, was initiated and planned by soldiers at the UFO coffeehouse, who used the space to hold meetings and distribute information.[29] In the days leading up to the planned pray-in, Blumsack and other soldiers distributed leaflets at bus stops, on post, and at the UFO, encouraging GIs to assemble at Chapel #1 to express their doubts about the war and to pray for peace. Word of the demonstration spread rapidly on post, and Blumsack was told by his commanding officer to cancel the event after army authorities objected to the word "doubt" printed on the flyers. The following day, Tuesday, February 13, 1968, a group of thirty-five GIs showed up at the chapel, unaware that the meeting had been canceled. Military police closed the post, surrounded the chapel, and ordered the crowd to disperse. Two soldiers kneeling in prayer were detained and charged with disturbing the peace.[30]

Although official charges against the meeting's leaders and participants were eventually dropped, the army found other ways to discipline the soldiers who had expressed antiwar views on post. Just a week after the pray-in, two of the men were sent to combat in Vietnam. Another was shipped to Korea. Blumsack himself was arrested two weeks after the chapel meeting, charged with a variety of driving violations, and, because he was too short to legally send into combat, eventually demoted to a lower pay grade.[31] The army authorities at Fort Jackson sent a strong message that antiwar activity would be met with severe retribution and that the military leadership had the seemingly unlimited power to disrupt the lives of soldiers who spoke out against its policies.

SUMMER OF SUPPORT: BUILDING A COFFEEHOUSE NETWORK

In the wake of the pray-in action and its fallout, Fred Gardner's GI coffeehouse concept finally captured the attention of leaders within some of the nation's prominent antiwar organizations. He began receiving calls and letters from activists who wanted to see it develop into a larger project, hoping to harness the energy of antiwar soldiers.[32] Gardner himself felt vindicated, excited that the "official" antiwar movement was interested in engaging with soldiers and in growing his coffeehouse idea. At the time, the National Mobilization Committee to End the War in Vietnam was one of the country's more well-funded and visible antiwar organizations. The "Mobe," as it was known, was in fact a loose coalition of more than 150 antiwar groups from around the country whose leadership had organized the Spring Mobilization demonstrations that had featured the debut of Vietnam Veterans Against the War. The Mobe was also responsible for an impressive set of actions on October 21, 1967, that brought more than 100,000 protesters to the Lincoln Memorial in the nation's capital. In one of the more memorable antiwar demonstrations of the Vietnam era, about 30,000 of these protesters made their way across the Potomac for a highly spirited march on the Pentagon later in the afternoon, an action immortalized in Norman Mailer's 1968 account *The Armies of the Night*.[33]

After the momentum gathered by the Pentagon event, Mobe leaders Dave Dellinger, Rennie Davis, and Tom Hayden sought to link their civilian antiwar activities with the rapidly developing GI movement. The UFO coffeehouse, in the news because of the chapel pray-in, seemed the perfect way to unite their antiwar principles with their desire to more directly engage with the military itself.[34] Mobe representatives visited the UFO coffeehouse in Columbia shortly after the pray-in made national headlines. They told Fred Gardner that they wanted to create a network of antiwar coffeehouses, just like the UFO, outside military bases around the country. These efforts would be kicked off by a "Summer of Support" campaign to help provide the publicity, fund-raising, and staff needed to sustain what they imagined would be a major support structure for a developing antiwar movement in the U.S. military. During the Mobe's visit to the UFO, Gardner helped the organization draft a press release that outlined an ambitious plan to expand his original coffeehouse idea:

> This summer, students and veterans will bring a new kind of support to GIs. By June 12, Summer of Support (SOS) plans to open coffeehouses, USOs for Peace, near all nine major US Army posts with training programs.
>
> The coffeehouses will be similar to the one in Columbia, S.C., where Ft. Jackson GIs met and planned the Feb. 13 pray-in at the base chapel. They will provide a place where anti-war GIs can get together, relax and talk about activities not reported in the Army—a place where they can air their gripes, plan and organize.
>
> In addition, SOS will offer day care centers for children of military personnel, legal counseling, theater, newspapers, rock concerts and academic programs. Entertainers like Judy Collins, the Jefferson

Airplane, Country Joe and the Fish and Phil Ochs will be invited to participate.

SOS is being sponsored by a group of veterans, students, journalists and entertainers who believe the US should withdraw from Vietnam. They feel that "it is the soldier who suffers most directly from the war and who has the most to gain from it coming to a fast, unambiguous end."[35]

The press release was published in antiwar newspapers and sent out as a fund-raising letter to New Left organizations and activists around the country, promoting the UFO coffeehouse as a model for the off-post support of antiwar soldiers.

The Mobe's coffeehouse announcement outlined the organizers' general philosophy on the coffeehouse network's appropriate relationship to GIs: "The coffee-houses are not designed to organize soldiers; they are designed to provide soldiers with a resource institution through which they can organize themselves, when they are ready. The qualities needed in coffee-house staff are not those of a political activist; they are those of friend and soda-jerk. Warmth, friendliness, openness, and a willingness to listen are the qualities needed to make soldiers feel at home and unthreatened in the coffeehouse. The coffeehouses give movement people an opportunity to make their rhetoric of fraternity real—but nothing more." Sensing the resistance that coffeehouses could face in military towns, Davis warned prospective staff that "any explicit proselytizing by movement people who worked there would be inappropriate and even threatening to the coffeehouse's continued existence."[36] Besides, he argued, proselytizing was not necessary; soldiers were the last group of Americans who needed to be educated on the impact of the war.

The June 1968 press release marked the beginning of a new phase in the coffeehouse network's development, with financial and material support coming from a host of different organizations within the national antiwar movement.[37] The most prominent of these organizations was the United States Servicemen's Fund (USSF), which spent millions of dollars over a period of six years in support of various GI coffeehouse projects.[38] The USSF was created in the last months of 1968 by Fred Gardner, Howard Levy, Dr. Benjamin Spock, Noam Chomsky, and other prominent antiwar activists. As the main umbrella organization gathering civilian support for the GI movement, the USSF exerted major influence on the direction of the coffeehouse network it intended to build, providing political direction, cultural support, and, perhaps most important, fund-raising for GI coffeehouses around the country.[39] The USSF's first major expansion of the GI coffeehouse network, in late 1968, set the ambitious goal of opening projects near all nine major army training posts within the United States.[40]

"IT'S OUR JOB TO LEND THEM SUPPORT": THE CHALLENGES OF ON-BASE ORGANIZING

As the USSF and other antiwar organizations envisioned building a larger, more politically active coffeehouse network, its leaders discovered some of the intense complicating factors involved with political activism among active-duty military service members.[41] One unavoidable reality had to be addressed: political work was extremely dangerous for GIs, who exposed themselves to significant risks by becoming active against the war. The army administrations of the late 1960s were particularly restrictive when it came to antiwar activity in the ranks. At U.S. Army posts throughout the world, regulations specifically forbade virtually all forms of political expression, including public assembly, distribution of literature, and the wearing of political symbols. The Uniform Code of Military Justice provided for several degrees of official punishment, including arrest and imprisonment, for those soldiers whose political activities were deemed "breaches of law and order."[42]

Beyond these formal regulations, though, an informal system of harassment and intimidation further reinforced the military's intolerance of political expression, particularly the antiwar variety, among the soldier rank and file.[43] As one historian-activist pointed out in 1975, there were many different ways that local posts dealt with dissent: "It would probably be safe to assert . . . that nearly every serviceman seriously attempting to resist war and injustice has suffered some sort of privation. Whether it be the loss of a security clearance, removal from a job, transfer to an isolated post, discharge under less than honorable conditions, or outright imprisonment, GI activists have paid a stiff price for their commitment. The certain knowledge of such consequences has deterred many would-be participants."[44]

The USSF's mission was further complicated by the transitory nature of service in the armed forces, particularly among the population of young soldiers most likely to engage in antiwar activities. GIs rarely stayed in one location for an extended period of time. The high degree of turnover made the task of creating lasting political institutions a difficult one. Even if active-duty soldiers were willing and able to take the risk of becoming politically active, the likelihood of their impending transfer or discharge meant that their effectiveness had a time limit.[45] This political impermanence was one of the key factors that groups like the USSF hoped to address by using civilian activists located in off-post coffeehouses to provide stability for a transient population of soldiers.

No one could be more aware of the difficulties and risks involved with GI political activism than Dr. Howard Levy, who served nearly three years in military prison for his refusal to provide medical training to Special Forces heading to Vietnam. Despite being incarcerated between 1967 and 1970, Levy remained politically engaged and active in the GI movement, even holding covert meetings with antiwar organizers while still imprisoned. Levy was instrumental in the formation of the USSF, helping raise funds for the opening of two "Support Our Soldiers" field offices in Oakland, California, and New York City in late 1968. He became an articulate spokesman for the civilian wing of the GI movement, penning numerous USSF newsletters and other communications, his comments appearing often in interviews throughout the underground and alternative press. Levy frequently emphasized, like Gardner, the importance of soldiers organizing themselves, with the civilian antiwar movement offering material and ideological support. "The GIs are taking the risks. We therefore feel that they should be running their own programs. It's our job to lend them support," he told a reporter.[46] Levy had a wide definition of what "civilian support" could mean, and his strong voice within the USSF helped guide the national coffeehouse movement to embrace a variety of strategies in its relationship to soldiers.

By mid-1969, the USSF had settled on a loose blueprint for the overall direction and purpose of the GI coffeehouse network: "educating GIs about the war and the nature of American society, bringing together GIs who are opposed or become opposed to the war and the brass and helping them form more cohesive political organizations and serving as a base out of which these organizations can operate."[47] But the organization also stressed the importance of maintaining a youth-oriented, alternative culture at GI coffeehouses: "a prerequisite to this kind of political organizing has been to provide the kind of music and general atmosphere in the coffeehouses which would attract the constituency in which the potential political GIs could be found."[48] The USSF was betting that a counterculture coffeehouse would attract the kind of young disaffected soldiers who could, with direction and support, become more active and informed antiwar GIs.

In addition to scheduling political presentations, usually in the form of guest speakers and films, civilian coffeehouse staff was expected to encourage and promote discussions among soldiers and other patrons afterward. These discussions were designed to duplicate the kinds of "rap sessions" that were nearly impossible for soldiers to hold on post and were meant to help GIs discover that they were not alone in their concerns and grievances. While the organization was careful to point out that "soldiers [should] be encouraged to develop their own thinking," it was clear that the USSF envisioned coffeehouse staff members as more than passive sources of information and coordinators of cultural activities; civilian staff were to serve as active political organizers working directly with GIs to build an antiwar movement within the military.[49]

As the coffeehouse network began to expand, the USSF's role in day-to-day operations was minimal; its main responsibility was providing financial and material backing for coffeehouses and related GI projects. According to the USSF's fund-raising letters, though, the high cost of opening and sustaining GI coffeehouses around the country was a complicated financial and logistical undertaking. In addition to opening costs (which included the purchase of furniture, legal and licensing fees, and security deposits), the USSF helped provide coffeehouses with paid entertainers, films, projectors, typewriters, mimeograph machines, and a near-constant supply of radical books and periodicals.[50] Particularly in the coffeehouse network's early years, the USSF's support was vital to the young activists who began cautiously stationing themselves in army towns around the country in the summer of 1968.

HIPPIES IN THE HEART OF TEXAS: THE OLEO STRUT OPENS IN KILLEEN

Josh Gould was twenty-three years old when he arrived in Killeen, Texas, in June 1968. A civil rights and peace activist, he had traveled around the country for several years, mainly working with college political organizations like the Student Nonviolent Coordinating Committee and Students for a Democratic Society. After briefly working at the UFO coffeehouse in Columbia, in the spring Gould had joined with twenty-one-year-old activist Janet ("Jay") Lockard in attempting to open a similar GI coffeehouse in Leesville, Louisiana, outside Fort Polk. Going it alone proved difficult, though, so when Gould and Lockard heard that Fred Gardner and a small group of friends had rented a storefront in Killeen and were turning it into another off-post counterculture and antiwar coffeehouse for soldiers stationed at Fort Hood, they immediately headed to Texas to join them.⁵¹ The two young activists, upon arriving in town, quickly recognized that Killeen, like other military towns, maintained a powerful connection to the American military establishment that stretched down into the very root structure of the town's history.

The story of Killeen, as the title of one local history suggests, is a "tale of two cities," one a tiny rural community centered almost entirely on agriculture, the other a bustling military town serving the needs of one of the largest army posts in the country. When Killeen was first settled in 1882, it functioned as a railroad depot just forty miles north of rapidly expanding Austin. A conglomerate of railroad companies sponsored a national media campaign, promoting Killeen as a central shipping point for goods like cotton, wool, and grain, attracting local farmers, small businessmen, and their families. By the turn of the twentieth century, the town had grown from a small shipping outpost to include six general stores, three cotton gins, three blacksmiths, two hardware stores, and a jeweler.⁵²

Killeen sustained a small population, never more than 2,000 people, for the first sixty years of its existence. The virtually homogeneous white Protestant community specifically discouraged settlement by blacks and Catholics, and Killeen remained a relatively insulated rural town until the Great Depression initiated a process of rapid evolution. Various New Deal public works projects expanded Killeen's physical infrastructure, and as roads, sewage systems, and larger highways were constructed, the city's population naturally increased. Perhaps more important for Killeen's future, though, the New Deal projects also cemented the city's friendly relationship with the federal government, a relationship that grew closer through the twentieth century. In 1942, Killeen became the site of a new army training base constructed to serve the demands of World War II. The hardship of the Depression made the idea of a new army camp attractive to many Killeen residents, who saw an opportunity for economic growth and stability.

The arrival of the U.S. Army dramatically transformed Killeen, ultimately initiating a wholly new chapter in the region's history. The construction of Camp Hood, as it was first called, "hit Killeen like a bolt of lightning" as the government purchased over half of the area's farms and trading centers, and virtually overnight a small agricultural economy became a military economy.⁵³ The need for farm service businesses like cotton gins, grain warehouses, and corn weighers was severely reduced, replaced by businesses that supported an exploding population of soldiers, construction workers, government employees, and their families who flooded into the city by the thousands through the

1940s and 1950s. By 1955, a population of 24,000 compelled the building of new schools, a hospital, and nearly 300 local businesses.[54]

Along with this dramatic expansion came an equally dramatic shift in Killeen's economic and cultural orientation. The town's fortunes, for better or worse, became inextricably tied to the presence of the U.S. military. As a local historian described the relationship, "the complete economic foundation of the town, its very reason for existence," had been "replaced by an economy dependent upon the federal government."[55] In the early years of Fort Hood, this fact was starkly demonstrated by a series of economic recessions that coincided with troop cutbacks during peacetime. The mid-1950s, for example, saw difficult times in Killeen, as the end of the Korean War hastened a severe downturn in military activity at Fort Hood. Business boomed again, however, in 1959, when the First Armored Division returned permanently to the post. The increased tensions of the Cold War indirectly provided Killeen with a lasting economic stability, which became even stronger as the Vietnam War developed through the 1960s. During the height of the war, Fort Hood housed a rotating population of more than 40,000 soldiers, and Killeen itself grew to include nearly 35,000 permanent residents. Killeen's small downtown commercial district increasingly oriented itself to serve the needs of Fort Hood GIs, as rows of dry cleaners (for uniforms), jewelry stores, pawn shops, and bookstores sprang up next to a movie theater, several pool halls, and a pinball arcade.[56] It was in this area of town that antiwar organizers decided, in 1968, to open Killeen's first counterculture coffeehouse based on the model created by Fred Gardner in Columbia, South Carolina.

When Gould and Lockard arrived in Killeen, Gardner and his friends had just rented an old TV repair shop at 101 Avenue D in the center of the commercial district. Gardner wanted the new arrivals to take over the project, freeing him to move on to other military towns to repeat the same pattern of organizing the coffeehouse's practical elements (like securing space and business licenses) before giving the coffeehouse over to a staff of volunteer antiwar activists. Within a week, Gould and Lockard were put in charge of designing, staffing, and managing the coffeehouse project in Killeen. After decorating the place with psychedelic "spinning colored lights," personality posters of celebrities like Raquel Welch, and a stage for live performances, the Killeen group decided on a name for the coffeehouse: the Oleo Strut, referring to the vertical shock absorber on the underside of a helicopter. The Strut, as it came to be known, hoped to absorb the shock of service in the Vietnam-era American military.[57]

The name was particularly appropriate for an establishment near Fort Hood, where 65 percent of the post's 40,000 soldiers were recent returnees from service in Vietnam.[58] Often referred to as "short-timers," these veterans had completed their required thirteen-month tours in Vietnam but still had months left in their overall service requirement and spent their remaining time hanging around American bases with little to keep them occupied. As the army itself soon recognized, short-timers were the soldiers most likely to engage in political activism against the war, and the staff of the Oleo Strut coffeehouse were eager to use these veterans' war experiences and ample free time to stimulate a more vigorous antiwar discourse at Fort Hood.

The Oleo Strut's grand opening celebration, held in Killeen's Condor Park on July 5, 1968, showed off the youthful counterculture and radical politics that characterized much of the coffeehouse phenomenon. Strut organizers, along with activists from the University of Texas Veterans' Committee (an Austin-based antiwar group), held a "love-in" that included folk and rock performances, antiwar speeches, and copious amounts of marijuana. Approximately 800 people attended the event, among them more than 200 soldiers from Fort Hood. By the end of the day, Killeen police arrived in riot gear and broke up the party, but the Oleo Strut coffeehouse and its organizers had succeeded in making a highly visible entrance onto the town's cultural scene.[59]

A few weeks after the Oleo Strut's opening festivities, an editorial titled "The Big Smear" appeared in the town's one local newspaper, the *Killeen Daily Herald*. The paper's staff disputed the coffeehouse's assumption that Fort Hood was teeming with dissident GIs and reminded citizens of the community's historical connection to the military base and wider ideological alignment with U.S. foreign policy: "We must not forget that this Central Texas fortress during World War II, the Korean War, and now the Vietnam War, has a proud record of achievement. The training instilled in thousands of troops has helped bring battlefield victories in the highest military tradition, and in the end, will help win the final battle. We must always remember that Fort Hood and Killeen are inseparable, and that the happiness, the sorrow, or the mission of one becomes that of the other."[60] By registering its disgust with the coffeehouse from the moment it opened, pitting it against the community's traditions and long-term interests, the town's newspaper helped ensure that the Oleo Strut would become a subject of significant local controversy.

That 200 soldiers would show up to an event billed as a "love-in" was a testament to Fort Hood's special status among soldiers of the era, many of whom were aware of the post's notoriety for extensive drug use and insubordination.

One reason for the post's unusually high levels of marijuana use was a case of environmental serendipity: the intoxicating plant grew naturally in large amounts throughout the area. As one GI reported, "It grows wild all around the base, so when you go out on tank maneuvers you just reach out and grab all you want, dry it, and start smoking."[61] The post was so well known among the military's growing number of regular pot smokers that in hip circles it earned the nickname "Fort Head."[62] The staff of the Oleo Strut coffeehouse hoped that the post's outlaw reputation could be channeled into a more coherent challenge to the local leadership and the larger military establishment.

Events like the Strut-sponsored love-in may have attracted a large crowd of soldiers and young people, but many Killeen residents were deeply offended by such public displays; some of them were moved to violence. Small bands of local vigilantes (often joined or supported by city police) regularly attacked the coffeehouse and its organizers in its early days. These groups mainly comprised Killeen high school students, who wreaked often alcohol-fueled havoc throughout town. Kicking off their campaign of terror against the Strut by smashing musical equipment at the love-in, the teenagers repeatedly broke the coffeehouse's front windows, stole the Strut's sign, and generally menaced the staff in the first weeks of the coffeehouse's existence. The activists working at the Strut initially took a nonviolent approach to the aggression, until local GIs convinced them to stock the store with baseball bats and a shotgun for self-defense. The attackers finally relented in their harassment after those on the staff displayed their willingness to fight back.[63]

Despite violent juveniles and other dangers, political activity organized by Fort Hood GIs began developing at the Oleo Strut coffeehouse throughout the summer of 1968. Private Bruce "Gypsy" Peterson began regularly leaving his post at Fort Hood to spend time at the coffeehouse, eventually founding and editing an underground antiwar newspaper for GIs, *Fatigue Press*, out of the Strut's back office. *Fatigue Press* formed a vital link between activists at the coffeehouse and soldiers at Fort Hood; Peterson, with the help of Strut staff, mimeographed hundreds of copies of the paper before smuggling them on post to covertly distribute them to fellow soldiers. Peterson's work as an underground newspaper editor caught the attention of post leadership, and he soon discovered that his actions had provoked military and city authorities to wage their own campaign of repression against him.

In the first weeks of August 1968, just two months after the first hand-drawn issues of *Fatigue Press* had been brought on post, Peterson began to find small bags of marijuana in his locker. Each time he discovered another bag, he threw it away, disturbed by the sense that he was being set up. Over the course of the next month, Killeen city police arrested Peterson for marijuana possession three different times. The final arrest occurred as Peterson stood in front of the Oleo Strut coffeehouse, where police claimed to have found a microscopic amount of marijuana mixed in with Peterson's pocket lint. Despite the lab technician later admitting that the evidence was completely destroyed upon examination, Peterson was convicted in military court and sentenced to eight years of hard labor at Leavenworth federal penitentiary.[64] The severe sentence failed to quell dissent at Fort Hood, however. *Fatigue Press* continued in Peterson's absence (he was released on appeal two years later), edited and published by a staff of volunteer soldiers at the Oleo Strut coffeehouse.[65]

By the end of the summer of 1968, the Oleo Strut had established firm roots in Killeen despite local resistance, and USSF organizers began looking into the possibility of establishing coffeehouses in other military towns. After sizing up several options, they set their sights on one of the largest and most critical areas of domestic military development in the United States: the Pacific Northwest. In Tacoma, Washington, just outside of Seattle, the Vietnam War was omnipresent, as the area's two major military bases (Fort Lewis army post and McChord Air Force Base) became central to the war effort. Unlike the army towns in which Gardner and others had opened the first GI coffeehouses, Tacoma carried a history of working-class radicalism that existed alongside, and within, its military-industrial development. As coffeehouse organizers soon discovered upon landing in town in late 1968, the mix of military service and left-wing activism that permeated the Pacific Northwest would provide a more welcoming environment for the kind of subversive institution they envisioned.

"GRIT CITY": FINDING FERTILE GROUND IN TACOMA

The town of Tacoma, Washington, was built around Commencement Bay, a large inlet off the Puget Sound that made the area a prime seaport for international trade. After the Northern Pacific Railway, the first transcontinental railroad in the northern United States, decided to locate its western terminus at Commencement Bay in 1873, Tacoma quickly grew into a small but booming port town. Fort Lewis's construction in 1917 secured the region as a permanent military installation and helped continue Tacoma's rapid expansion. Due to its high concentration of working-class residents, beginning with the railroad workers of the nineteenth century and continuing with the longshoremen of the twentieth, Tacoma had a long history of blue-collar labor organizing, earning its image as the West's "Grit City."[66]

Tacoma's Fort Lewis army post served a central role in the Pacific theater of World War II and later evolved into a critical training and processing center for American troops as the United States escalated its military campaign in Southeast Asia through the 1960s. In May 1966, military officials established a $6.3 million "Army Personnel Center" at Fort Lewis that ultimately handled the induction of more than 2.3 million soldiers before closing in 1972. In addition to processing new recruits, the post was also transformed into the army's central training grounds for Vietnam combat, with GIs participating in simulated war games on a meticulously constructed 15,000-acre "Vietnam Village" complex featuring thatched-roof "hootches" and American soldiers role-playing as the Viet Cong.[67]

Though Fort Lewis in particular developed into one of the U.S. Army's most important domestic bases of operations throughout the Vietnam War, the entire Washington State area in fact played a critical role in the military's overall war effort. The region's natural, human, and economic resources made an ideal location for military activity of all kinds. The Puget Sound area, which included both Tacoma and nearby Seattle, held high strategic value, and during the 1960s all four branches of the military had active bases that took advantage of the region's deepwater bays and vast swaths of undeveloped land. In addition to Fort Lewis, the area housed McChord Air Force Base, Fort Lawton army base, Pier 91 Naval Station, Sand Point Naval Air Station, and the Puget Sound Naval Shipyard. All of these bases contributed to a ubiquitous military presence in Washington, a presence that became even more pronounced as the Vietnam War brought an influx of military personnel to the state beginning in 1964.[68] The impact of the Vietnam War on Fort Lewis was felt most strikingly by the losses sustained by its Fourth Infantry Division, a group of more than 70,000 soldiers who had been stationed, in rotation, at the Lewis base beginning in 1956. The Fourth Infantry was called to combat duty in Vietnam in July 1966. Over the course of four years, the Tacoma-based division lost 16,844 men to death and injury before being relieved of service during Nixon's initial troop withdrawal in early 1970.[69]

Tacoma's deep involvement in the operation of the Vietnam War, including the Fourth Infantry's losses, made for a strong local connection to military issues. In many ways, the war itself became a kind of hometown story, as local newspapers promoted Fort Lewis's commitment to the war effort as a point of particular strength and pride. As was true of other American military towns, Tacoma's business community directly benefited from the region's identification with nearby military bases. This identification was frequently celebrated and reinforced by Congressman Floyd V. Hicks, who represented Kitsap, King, and Pierce Counties (which included Tacoma) and served on the House Armed Services Committee from 1964 to 1975. Hicks was a tireless promoter of the military's presence in the Tacoma area, and his efforts to convince the federal government to expand military allocations to Fort Lewis contributed to the local economy's dependence on the army post. Even though the Vietnam War would ultimately inflict heavy casualties on the men and women who passed through Fort Lewis, for Tacoma's business and political elite the war was an opportunity for increased profit and local prestige.[70]

Tacoma's social and political atmosphere was also shaped by its proximity to Seattle, a major center for New Left and counterculture activity. A *New York Times* reporter, visiting Tacoma in 1969, highlighted its location along a corridor of West Coast highways well traveled by young radical activists, noting Tacoma's high population of activists "drawn from the virtually endless supply of New Politics leftists around San Francisco Bay."[71] In addition to the pipeline of radicals from Northern California, many activists also emerged from the University of Washington's Seattle campus. During the 1960s, UW-Seattle experienced significant growth in both its physical infrastructure and its faculty and student composition; the tenure of university President Charles Odegaard contributed to a dramatic expansion of the institution's operating budget and national prestige, and by the end of his term the student population had more than doubled, from 16,000 in 1958 to more than 34,000 in 1973. The influx of new students also helped bring about a rising level of political activism, most notably the establishment of a large and influential chapter of Students for a Democratic Society, which often stood at the center of a lively youth antiwar movement in and around the Washington state area.[72]

In addition to Students for a Democratic Society, other radical organizations more closely associated with the "Old Left" maintained a significant presence in the Pacific Northwest in the late 1960s, and it was the influence of these groups, most prominently the Socialist Workers Party and its youth corollary, the Young Socialist Alliance (YSA), that initiated a more direct relationship between the antiwar movement and American soldiers.[73] In Seattle, the Young Socialist Alliance's relatively small membership nevertheless aggressively promoted GI activism as part of the Socialist Workers Party's larger political strategy. To alliance members, students could more effectively stimulate revolutionary social change by directing their movement toward the military's working class: "Our work in support of GI antiwar fighting will give our movement an avenue to real POWER for the first time."[74]

Inspired by the growing antiwar resistance from within the military, evidenced in well-publicized cases such as the trial of the "Fort Jackson Eight," the small but active Socialist Workers Party chapters in Seattle helped lay the groundwork for coffeehouse organizers' plans to build a movement at Fort Lewis. In the fall of 1968, student activists at the University of Washington, working directly with the Young Socialist Alliance and other antiwar organizations, initiated one of the country's first direct campaigns to link the civilian Left with the varied acts of resistance then permeating the armed forces. By forming the GI-Civilian Alliance for Peace, young antiwar organizers hoped to demonstrate their solidarity with young GIs alienated from military authority and the war in Vietnam.

The formation of the GI-Civilian Alliance for Peace caught the attention of Fred Gardner and other national coffeehouse organizers. Because of the early activities of the alliance (which included the creation of a GI underground newspaper, *Counterpoint*, and a near-constant presence outside the gates of Fort Lewis), in addition to the robust antiwar movement taking place at the nearby University of Washington, Tacoma was, more than any other military town in the country, primed for the creation of an antiwar coffeehouse.[75]

"MOM AND DAD'S CANDY STORE":
EARLY DAYS AT THE SHELTER HALF

The Tacoma coffeehouse was modeled after the other Summer of Support coffeehouses then establishing their own roots in Columbia, South Carolina, and Killeen, Texas. Honoring the practice of co-opting a military term for their project's name, organizers christened the coffeehouse the Shelter Half, the name derived from an army term that referred to a small piece of sticky canvas (a "shelter half"), carried by all soldiers, which was effectively useless unless two soldiers joined them together to form a two-man tent. By naming the coffeehouse after this particular piece of equipment, its organizers hoped to evoke a sense of strength through solidarity and cooperation. Of course, the coffeehouse would also serve as a literal "shelter" from the particular military culture at Fort Lewis, and, like other GI coffeehouses, the organizers covered its walls with personality posters of counterculture celebrities such as Allen Ginsberg, Muhammad Ali, Che Guevara, and even Charlie Chaplin. Serving coffee, soft drinks, and inexpensive meals made from a small kitchen, the

Shelter Half initially presented itself as a hip environment where military men were welcome to relax, listen to music, and talk with friends.

In its early months the Shelter Half went out of its way to project a GI-friendly atmosphere. An elaborate free Christmas dinner, advertised by leaflets at Fort Lewis's gates and in the local underground press, was an early success; about twenty GIs from post came to share a meal and conversation with their radical civilian hosts. In a handwritten letter to the Shelter Half staff, a GI later expressed his gratitude for the feast, explaining that he and a friend had been driving aimlessly around Tacoma on Christmas Day, tired and hungry, when they stumbled upon the coffeehouse: "Here waiting for us [at the Shelter Half] we find free coffee, good music, something to read & heat too . . . Wow! Q: What else could a G.I. want? A: Not have to ride back to Ft. Lewis and eat their shit. And their food too. Well we didn't have to, the great people at the Shelter Half solved the problem by serving a Christmas dinner that couldn't be beat. Wine, fruit, nuts the whole bit. Gratis, free, on the house, on the good half. For all this, all I can offer is our thanks."[76]

With the holiday dinner serving as a kind of formal introduction to Tacoma's military community, the Shelter Half project entered the new year, 1969, with a certain amount of local word-of-mouth and a growing number of curious servicemen showing up to sample the atmosphere. This burst of popularity led directly to increased political activism in Tacoma. After visiting the coffeehouse and learning that it supported a local branch of GIs United, an air force pilot identified only as "W. R." felt compelled to offer a financial contribution:

> Peace Brothers—
> Wandered into the coffee house last night and I heard you just formed a GIs United. So am sending $10.00 to help out and plan to attend your next meeting. Hope you can use the money to put out some more copies of leaflets or such. We really need to spread the word. I'm on McChord and I just found out about you guys this week. I'm sure I know many more guys who would dig a group like yours, so I'll spread the word. Keep up the good work.[77]

Within the first few months of business in Tacoma, the Shelter Half gained the attention of its target audience of GIs, service members, and military veterans from around the Tacoma area, and its organizers discovered that a significant portion of this population was willing to lend its support, in various ways, to the operation of the coffeehouse itself.

Stan Anderson, then a twenty-two-year-old army veteran who had been stationed at Fort Lewis, became the Shelter Half's first manager and unofficial spokesperson in 1968. When a local newspaper reporter visited the coffeehouse during its first week of operation in Tacoma, Anderson explained the establishment's function in terms that echoed Fred Gardner's original vision of coffeehouses as open discussion spaces: "We want to provide a free atmosphere where military personnel can associate with students and other civilians. The Shelter Half will provide an open forum for the exchange of ideas, free from any restrictions on political or ideological discussion.... The direction we take locally will be decided by the people who use the place." Anderson acknowledged that the coffeehouse had an undeniable "peace orientation" and stressed that, since the expression of antiwar opinions by active-duty personnel was often met with severe harassment and reprimand, the coffeehouse could offer a safe place for those soldiers alienated by the sometimes narrow cultural and political environment both on post and in the string of local bars that dotted Tacoma's downtown. In Anderson's view, the Shelter Half coffeehouse could begin to address the alienation many young soldiers (such as Anderson himself) experienced in the small military town. That alienation, Anderson pointed out, was often exacerbated by the Vietnam War's deep unpopularity among young people throughout the nation: "When I was at Fort Lewis, there were few activities that brought me into contact with members of the local community. It really boiled down to a choice of staying on the post or making the bar rounds.... I felt the people of Tacoma were interested in soldiers only because of the money they spend here. I had nothing here I could relate to and felt like a second-class citizen. The war, though, has resulted in the drafting of many students and college graduates who understand and want the sort of dialogue that a coffeehouse can offer. We want to give these people a place where they can feel at home."[78]

As the Shelter Half gained notoriety in Tacoma and surrounding areas, civilian antiwar activists began heading to the Pacific Northwest to help out. Playwright and antiwar activist Barbara Garson had first heard about the GI coffeehouse concept from her friendship with Fred Gardner in Berkeley, California, in 1968. Garson had just come off a recent success with the political satire *MacBird!*, a controversial play in verse that cast the Johnson presidency and the Kennedy family in a subversive adaptation of Shakespeare's *Macbeth*. After overseeing a successful year-long run of *MacBird* at the Village Gate Theater in New York City in 1967, Garson returned to the San Francisco Bay area, eager to find new ways to contribute to the antiwar effort. When she heard about the Shelter Half's need for new staff members, Garson moved up the coast to Tacoma in early 1969 to work at the coffeehouse and help build the GI movement at Fort Lewis.

Though she very much opposed the Vietnam War and wanted to work to stop it, for most of the 1960s Garson felt alienated from the organized antiwar movement. Like Gardner, she envisioned herself as providing material and spiritual support for a movement led and organized by GIs rather than by civilians, later recalling her distaste for the way civilian left-wing activists often approached GI organizing: "The last thing they were interested in was stories about GIs standing up for themselves. And that's what I was there for: the American people would be standing up for themselves. I actually thought that that [direct kind of] antiwar work was a step back. I thought the best way to be involved in the antiwar effort was to be involved with American people fighting for themselves."[79] Beyond the opportunity to interact with GIs, one of the more appealing aspects of working at the Shelter Half, to Garson, was that the coffeehouse provided an ideal environment in which to simultaneously work and raise her young daughter. "It was a very good place to work with a child. You could be in political work, doing important things, and yet be separated less from your child than if you were a stay-at-home mother. And for my daughter, it was like being in Mom and Dad's candy store."[80]

Though Garson may have characterized the Shelter Half as a "candy store," to many of Tacoma's citizens the coffeehouse's intentions appeared sinister, even threatening. Among these citizens was the director of the city's Department of Tax and License, D. H. McLellan, who began investigating the Shelter Half almost immediately after it opened its doors on October 4, 1968. Over the course of its first months in business, local police visited the coffeehouse on several occasions, presumably inspecting for various code violations. On February 6, 1969, two Tacoma police officers physically removed a pair of young boys (aged fifteen and eleven) for playing a coin-operated foosball machine set up in the Shelter Half's recreation room. Stan Anderson and another member of the coffeehouse staff, Miranda Bergman, were arrested and charged with "contributing to the delinquency of a minor." The next day, McLellan drafted a letter to the Shelter Half staff that announced his intentions to revoke the coffeehouse's business license. Defending his decision to a *New York Times* reporter, McLellan insisted that the city had the right to deny licenses to "any person believed to desire such license to enable him to practice some dishonest or immoral act." While McLellan did not itemize the Shelter Half's perceived "dishonest" or "immoral" acts, he evidently spoke for many

Tacoma officials and residents when he insisted that the Shelter Half's operators "think different than some of us."[81]

When Anderson and Bergman returned to the coffeehouse after being released from city jail, they discovered that their car had been set on fire, the wreckage left smoldering in its parking space in front of the coffeehouse. Though the coffeehouse staff never discovered the precise circumstances behind the car's burning, the sight of the destroyed vehicle seemed like one more sign that, only months after arriving in town, the Shelter Half had made some determined enemies in Tacoma. Like the other GI movement organizers then establishing coffeehouse projects in military towns around the United States, the Shelter Half staff refused to allow local resistance to deter them from their mission. As 1968 turned to 1969, the Summer of Support had successfully set up three major coffeehouse projects. For the organizers at these projects, it was time to settle in to the real work: building a political movement of civilians and GIs against the war in Vietnam.

Getting Together

Political Activism at GI Coffeehouses

> Coffeehouses were the first form used to provide a place where active-duty servicemen and women could congregate in a military town without having that old gnawing feeling that you were being ripped off for your money. When public attention was first focused on the new attitudes among service people, and the developing struggle against the war within the military, coffeehouses were often pointed to as the visible symbol of that movement.
>
> About Face! The U.S. Servicemen's Fund Newsletter 2, no. 1 (November 1971)

"GIS UNITED": THE UFO AND THE FORT JACKSON EIGHT

In Columbia, South Carolina, where Fred Gardner had opened the UFO coffeehouse before leaving town to open others, the GI movement in and around Fort Jackson continued to gain momentum throughout 1968. Gardner and other activists knew the coffeehouse had struck a nerve when, shortly after the UFO gained popularity among GIs, Fort Jackson opened its own "counterculture" coffeehouse, decorated with posters of Hollywood stars (including Sophia Loren) and hosting folk singers who performed live.[1] GI and civilian organizers were both amused and encouraged by this development and viewed the army's attempt to create a hip hangout on post as a sure sign that their movement was gaining traction. Indeed, within a year of its opening, the UFO coffeehouse became involved in one of the GI movement's most explosive cases. In the early months of 1969, a group of antiwar soldiers on post challenged the military's right to restrict the constitutional liberties of active-duty soldiers. The case of the Fort Jackson Eight, as it became known, gained national media attention. The UFO coffeehouse played a key role in the case, providing both an organizational base and material support for the soldiers in their struggle against Fort Jackson authorities.[2]

The case began when a young black activist named Joe Miles, drafted and sent for training at Fort Jackson, arrived in town in January 1969. At his draft induction, Miles made it clear that he was an activist in the antiwar movement and a member of the Young Socialist Alliance, writing a letter indicating that he would obey all orders and regulations of the army while simultaneously using every legal opportunity to express his political views. True to his word, Miles began organizing black GIs at Fort Jackson the same week he arrived, forming a group called GIs United Against the War in Vietnam.

During the first few months of 1969, GIs United Against the War in Vietnam became highly visible at Fort Jackson and in Columbia. Participants held regular meetings at the UFO coffeehouse, finding its space especially suitable for the kinds of large group gatherings that were virtually impossible to sustain on post.[3] The main thrust of their activity was to circulate letters and petitions, hoping to demonstrate wide on-base opposition to the war and support for the individual GI's right to express that opposition. The group's "Statement of Aims," which was distributed at Fort Jackson and other army training posts, captures the organization's efforts to appeal to a wide constituency: "Do citizens in uniform have the protection of the First Amendment? Can they meet and discuss the war in Vietnam, even take positions on it? Others, even Congressmen and Senators, oppose the war; can the men required to fight it not legally do the same?"[4] In their public pronouncements, members of GIs United declared a straightforward, civil liberties–centered position that was effective in winning the support of a large number of soldiers at Fort Jackson.

On March 20, 1969, little more than a year after the chapel pray-in had brought together 35 antiwar soldiers at Fort Jackson, GIs United held a meeting outside a barracks that included nearly 200 soldiers. Organization members Jose Rudder and Andrew Pulley addressed the crowd while soldiers leaning out of dormitory windows raised clenched fists and shouted words of support. The increasingly raucous assembly eventually dispersed without major incident, but the following day Fort Jackson authorities labeled it a "riot" and arrested nine leaders of the GIs United organization, bringing them up on charges that included disrespect, holding an illegal demonstration, and disobeying orders.[5] The group was reduced to eight after it was revealed that GIs United member Private John Huffman had been working as an army informer. Placing an informer in GIs United indicated the level of concern the Fort Jackson group had created within the military establishment.[6] This revelation, along with the significant media publicity given the movement at Fort Jackson (including a live on-base interview of GIs United members featured on NBC's *Huntley-Brinkley Report*), led to a public relations and legal embarrassment for army officials, who in June dropped all charges against the remaining defendants and instead attempted to hasten their quiet exits from the military.[7]

Apart from being a significant victory for the GI movement, its civilian supporters, and the soldiers themselves, the fact that the army dropped all charges against the Fort Jackson Eight also signaled an important shift in how the military handled internal dissent. Just three years earlier, in 1966, the average GI activist convicted in military court was sentenced to forty-five months of hard labor. Howard Levy's three-year sentence for refusal to train medical staff had been one notable example.[8] The case of the Fort Jackson Eight was a major landmark in a continuum of events from 1967 to 1969. Those in the GI movement, together with civilian antiwar activists at the UFO coffeehouse, engaged the national media in their campaign, creating public and legal pressure for the army to reduce the harassment and imprisonment of soldiers who spoke against the war. Marveling at the group's rapid success at gaining widespread public support, influential antiwar activist (and the Socialist Workers Party's 1968 presidential candidate) Fred Halstead noted that the Fort Jackson Eight had paid "careful attention to what ordinary Americans would think of their actions, getting news out to the massive antiwar movement, and appealing to the civil-liberties traditions which are taken seriously by millions of Americans."[9] By focusing their defense on one issue, their right as American citizens to discuss the war in Vietnam, the Fort Jackson Eight won sympathy from a large section of the American public.[10]

The UFO coffeehouse was instrumental in the group's victory, providing meeting space, access to equipment like mimeograph machines, and networks of civilian supporters. While Joe Miles, Jose Rudder, Andrew Pulley, and other core leaders of GIs United had been activists before stepping foot in the UFO coffeehouse, the UFO's protected environment and its staff's access to funds, lawyers, and media outlets immeasurably helped the group's efforts to avoid military prison.¹¹ The army was clearly done dealing with Joe Miles, though. Immediately after the Fort Jackson Eight case was dismissed, Miles was shipped, on three hours' notice, to North Carolina's Fort Bragg, where he frustrated military authorities by establishing yet another chapter of GIs United before finally being redeployed in October to Anchorage, Alaska, the most remote army post in North America.¹²

"RIOT CONTROL? HELL NO!" THE FORT HOOD 43 AND RICHARD CHASE SHAKE UP KILLEEN

Echoing the UFO coffeehouse's successful role in the Fort Jackson Eight case, the Oleo Strut coffeehouse near Fort Hood in Killeen, Texas, became involved in a similarly precedent-setting case that tested the limits of political expression in the U.S. Army. Political energy among GIs had accelerated dramatically after the Oleo Strut coffeehouse opened its doors in 1968. In Killeen, though, the explosion of GI activism took on a particularly intense racial tone. A significant number of the post's population of black soldiers had begun organizing their own movement in the summer of 1968, reacting to national events with increasing anger and resistance. Black soldiers at Fort Hood were under a particular and immediate set of pressures that summer. Riots had erupted in black communities in more than 100 American cities in the wake of Martin Luther King Jr.'s assassination in April. Thousands of American troops were dispatched to quell the violence throughout the year, with Fort Hood becoming the main training and deployment base for riot control duty.¹³ Black soldiers, many of whom had recently returned from Vietnam, were especially angry, and increasing numbers resented their role in what the army called "civil disturbance control."¹⁴

The resentment felt by many black soldiers at Fort Hood first peaked in late August 1968 as the base made preparations to send soldiers to Chicago during the Democratic Party's national convention. After the Tet Offensive in Vietnam in January had laid waste to his constant claim of "victory around the corner," Lyndon B. Johnson made the decision not to pursue another presidential term, throwing the party into disarray over the war issue. Chicago's mayor Richard Daley, imagining massive numbers of marauding antiwar protesters descending on the city, promised to keep order by any means necessary, and Illinois governor Samuel H. Shapiro declared his support. In addition to troops from the Illinois National Guard, soldiers from Fort Hood were to be mobilized and sent to Chicago for riot control duty.

In the days leading up to the convention, black soldiers at Fort Hood began to organize in opposition to these orders. A group of sixty black soldiers assembled at Fort Hood on the night of August 23, drew up a list of grievances, and discussed whether they should refuse their orders to deploy to Chicago. Private Guy Smith, a Vietnam combat veteran, describing the mood of the gathering, recalled that "a lot of black GIs knew what the thing [in Chicago] was going to be about and they weren't going to go and fight their own people."[15] The meeting went on through the night, to the consternation of military authorities, and when forty-three men remained in the morning, all of them were arrested by military police.[16]

Organizers at the Oleo Strut coffeehouse immediately leapt into action to support the arrested soldiers, helping mount the group's defense and media strategy. In addition to providing a safe meeting space, the coffeehouse staff raised funds to hire a civilian lawyer and publicized the soldiers' situation in *Fatigue Press* and other underground media outlets. The case of the Fort Hood 43, as it became known, was another instance in which army authorities were caught off guard by the amount of publicity and sympathy given the defendants.[17] The case was prominent in the mainstream press for over a year as the various courts-martial progressed for the men who faced dishonorable discharges and in some cases prison time. The publicity brought further attention to the growing resentment toward riot control duty expressed by American soldiers and helped reveal the military's significant internal problems with morale and insubordination.[18]

For Josh Gould and the staff of the Oleo Strut, the lead-up to the highly anticipated Chicago convention provided an opportunity to express solidarity with black soldiers who had resisted riot control deployment. A group of white soldiers who regularly visited the Strut and who were among the 6,000 Fort Hood troops ordered to Chicago had the idea to wear stickers on their helmets that would show that they were on the "side" of the demonstrators, despite their service in the military. The sticker itself, which depicted a white hand giving the peace sign, backed by a clenched black fist, employed the specific political iconography of the era while hinting at some of the underlying tension and division within the antiwar movement.[19] Gould himself planned to drive to Chicago to help distribute the stickers and spread word to antiwar demonstrators about their symbolic significance.

Three hours before his plane left for Chicago, though, Gould drove to the Oleo Strut for a final visit. On the way, he was pulled over by Killeen police for making an illegal right turn. The police searched his car, claimed to find "grains" of marijuana in the vehicle's floor carpets, and arrested him. He was held in the Killeen city jail for eight days, through the duration of the convention in Chicago, until the police admitted that no marijuana was found in the car after all. Gould was released the day after the convention concluded and suspected (though could not prove) that the timing of his arrest had been orchestrated to disrupt his political activities.[20]

Despite the Oleo Strut staff's attempts to reach out to radical black soldiers at Fort Hood through the summer of 1968, significant racial problems among soldiers posed barriers to the kind of unity they hoped to build. Physical altercations between black and white soldiers were commonplace on post, both in the barracks and in the stockade. A series of fights at Fort Hood in the spring of 1969 eventually escalated into what authorities characterized as "race riots" in April. Amid the increased racial animosity and violence, the coffeehouse staff redoubled its efforts to promote solidarity among soldiers of different races, inviting a group of black soldiers to the Strut in hopes of brokering some kind of racial peace. As one staff member explained, "We talked about bringing together a large group of EMs (200–300), black, brown and white[,] to sign a peace treaty amongst themselves, which would recognize the hostilities and would serve to focus attention on a common enemy."[21] The groups eventually agreed upon a meeting at the coffeehouse in July 1969.

The black soldiers who came to the meeting were part of a group who identified with the "5%" movement, a radical black Islamic organization that had begun in Harlem in 1964.[22] According to Oleo Strut staff, the Five Percenters, as they referred to themselves, had a drastically different perspective on the racial situation at Fort Hood. According to a Strut staff member, "The specific group of blacks we talked to made it clear to us that because of the anti-white feelings of most blacks on post (which did not distinguish between EM and sergeant, between individual racism and institutional racism) . . . there could be no cooperation or alliance between black and white. In fact, the riot that we [Strut staff] and most whites dreaded was viewed as beneficial by the blacks, their first chance to strike back."[23] After the July 1969 meeting, the staff and GI activists at the Oleo Strut recognized that organizing black and white soldiers into a single unified movement would be a difficult, if not impossible, undertaking. "We finally dropped the idea," a follow-up report stated, "and concentrated on 1) serving as a resource place for the black organizers—literature, books etc.; 2) continuing to talk to white guys on a one to one basis, mainly about racism. We are also intending to start a literature campaign on fort. The forthcoming issue of the *Fatigue Press* is going to be a special Racism issue."[24] Alongside these educational efforts, coffeehouse staff continued to seek ways to address racism on post in more tangible ways.

Twenty-six-year-old private Richard Chase had been drafted and assigned to the Second Armored Division at Fort Hood in January 1969. Chase was ordered to participate in "Operation Garden Plot," Fort Hood's training program for urban riot control. Before beginning his training, he wrote a letter to his commanding officer and first sergeant, explaining his personal and political objections to riot control duty: "Riot control is the way guys in the Army are used by the government against people struggling for valid demands. I refuse to be used against people I support."[25] After reading his letter, authorities pulled him from training in Operation Garden Plot and gave him a job as an office clerk. In June, Chase began to regularly visit the Oleo Strut and quickly became one of the coffeehouse's most tireless GI organizers.

Chase talked to other GIs, both on post and at the Oleo Strut, about the Vietnam War and the soldiers' right to dissent. He organized petitions, assisted with the operation of the coffeehouse, and helped write, publish, and distribute *Fatigue Press*.[26] As his earlier letter indicated, Chase did not hide his antiwar orientation, and over the summer of 1969 authorities at Fort Hood began to pay closer attention to his activities. On September 11, he received direct orders to report to riot control training: "I was given the order by my commanding officer, who knew that I wouldn't comply because of my beliefs and political activity. The order was given to try to end my involvement in the GI movement."[27] When he rejected the order, Chase's commanding officer read him court-martial charges for refusing duty and sentenced him to "pre-trial confinement" in Fort Hood's stockade. According to Chase, his stay in the army's prison, while he awaited trial, was a particularly brutal experience; he was beaten by guards on four separate occasions and repeatedly placed in solitary confinement.[28]

In the months leading up to his trial, GI and civilian activists organized support for Chase, forming the Richard Chase Defense Committee to raise funds for legal defense and to publicize his case. The Oleo Strut coffeehouse was the center of the "Free Richard Chase" campaign, as organizers saw the case as another chance to unite white and black soldiers against the deeply unpopular program of riot control training at Fort Hood. Strut staff members created and circulated a petition demanding Chase's release and the end of riot control training at Fort Hood. More than 100 soldiers (both black and white), a majority of Chase's company at Fort Hood, signed the petition.

The Chase trial, which centered on the issue of riot control, created a significant amount of political momentum and media attention for the GI movement at Fort Hood. The defense committee sponsored several local rallies and events to demonstrate support for Chase and activist GIs, with prominent antiwar veterans speaking and folk and rock musicians performing at the Oleo Strut. Many Fort Hood GIs were present in the courtroom throughout Chase's trial and showed their support with clenched fists and peace signs. Richard Chase's act of resistance and the accompanying press coverage revealed that riot control training was not just hated by a small group of radical black soldiers but was in fact unpopular among a wide section of soldiers on post.[29]

Despite concerted efforts, led by the Oleo Strut coffeehouse, to have charges against him dropped, Richard Chase was convicted in military court on December 20, 1969, and sentenced to two years of hard labor at Leavenworth.[30] Although the defense committee failed to achieve its specific objectives (freeing Chase and ending riot control training), the case was a significant milestone in the development of antiwar activism at Fort Hood and provided activists with an organizational base from which they hoped to build an even larger movement. Most of all, the case signaled the possibility for greater racial unity at Fort Hood, as soldiers of all colors began to question being part of the government's first line of defense against the unrest breaking out in American cities. A staff member of the Oleo Strut explained that, even long after the trial was over, Chase's imprisonment continued to resonate with GIs as a symbol of the fight to end programs like Operation Garden Plot. Over the next few years, "when a GI demanded 'free Richard Chase' he was in essence demanding an end to riot control."[31]

THE OLEO STRUT DRAWS NATIONAL ATTENTION

With the momentum from the Chase trial, the Oleo Strut coffeehouse continued to attract more GIs from Fort Hood throughout 1969 and 1970, many of whom became involved in the publication of Fort Hood's increasingly popular underground GI newspaper. A July 1970 issue of *Fatigue Press* lists the names of ten active-duty Fort Hood soldiers as just "some of the GIs" working on newspaper staff. That anonymous attribution was not an affectation. For the active-duty soldiers who frequented the Oleo Strut and carried copies of *Fatigue Press*, their activism made them extremely vulnerable to institutional harassment of all kinds. They took many steps to minimize the dangers. Because the GI movement had, by 1970, existed for several years, organizers had developed a more sophisticated approach to publication and distribution of underground literature, learning from their fellow activists' experience with military repression. The lessons in survival came "at the cost of considerable harassment, courts-martial, and transfers to Vietnam," but over time organizers became much savvier about their activities. In 1970, the pacifist *WIN* magazine published a guide for GIs working on newspaper projects. The author, a Marine lance corporal, stressed that *writing* antiwar articles was protected by free speech, but *distribution* was murkier legal territory. Depending on the judgment of his local supervisors, any GI caught distributing literature could be subject to prosecution. *WIN* magazine urged GIs to either distribute newspapers covertly or employ civilian support networks (such as coffeehouses) for distribution.[32] Despite these warnings, GIs personally smuggled hundreds of copies of *Fatigue Press* and other underground publications from the Oleo Strut's back office to the army post at Fort Hood throughout the later years of the Vietnam War.

Dave Cline, stationed at Fort Hood after being wounded in Vietnam, became one of *Fatigue Press*'s most active promoters on post. He later described the sometimes harrowing experience of bringing antiwar newspapers into what he considered enemy territory:

> The way we would distribute literature is: We'd go on hits through the base and go through the barracks late at night and put them on wall lockers, put the papers on bunks, and stuff like that. We'd do hits and do an area and get through quick. We handed them out at gates and in the town. I was questioned by military authorities on a number of occasions. They would do wall locker searches. You could have anything you wanted in your locker. I had all sorts of shit... *LA Free Press*, underground papers, a book on Buddhism, radical books, stuff like that. [But] if they found more than one piece of literature in your wall locker, they could charge you with distribution of literature.[33]

On one occasion, Cline's commanding officer entered the barracks and demanded to search his locker. The officer carried a shotgun with a bayonet attached to the barrel and pointed the weapon at Cline as military police dug through his belongings. The tense confrontation reflected the vicious, personal tone of division among soldiers on base, with the Vietnam War serving as the fulcrum of a whole set of tensions and frustrations:

> I'm standing at attention and he's telling me shit like he hopes he sees me when he gets out of the service. I was responding, but in a way that I couldn't get in trouble. I said "I hope I see you too, sir." He started talking about the Viet Cong. I said, "I fought the Viet Cong, sir. I was wounded on several occasions." He's waving the bayonet in my face. I knew he wasn't going to stab me, because there were witnesses. He eventually turned and stormed out because they couldn't find more than one copy of any of the literature. We were careful about that. We were organizers.[34]

The dangers for activist soldiers at Fort Hood were not limited to overzealous authorities. As the Oleo Strut coffeehouse became more widely known in Killeen as a gathering place for antiwar radicals and local hippies, some Killeen residents directed aggression and anger at its staff and customers. Most of this harassment came from juvenile delinquents and took the form of obnoxious but relatively minor pranks: broken windows, stolen property, and thrown beer bottles.[35] On a few occasions, however, the threat of physical violence became much more serious.

On October 3, 1969, a group of more than twenty Fort Hood GIs piled into six separate cars and started the five-hour drive to Houston to participate in a peace rally in the city's Hermann Park. Shortly after leaving Killeen city limits, a vehicle pulled alongside the caravan's lead car and opened fire with automatic weapons, blowing out the tires and damaging the engine before speeding off. The shaken soldiers, determined to attend the rally, returned to Killeen, informed Texas Rangers of their situation, and obtained permission to carry one weapon per vehicle for self-defense on their way to Houston. When they returned to the Oleo Strut coffeehouse the following day, the GIs found on the front window of the damaged car a sticker that read "The Knights of the Ku Klux Klan are watching you."[36]

Despite this intimidation, by the fall of 1969, a little more than a year after opening, the Oleo Strut had gained national recognition as the home base for a rising antiwar movement among soldiers at Fort Hood. The wider GI movement had also evolved dramatically, from a few isolated cases in the mid-1960s to a larger and more organized national phenomenon in the late 1960s, and mainstream media coverage accompanied this growth. In 1968, major national publications like *Look*, *Life*, and *Esquire* magazines featured cover stories on soldier antiwar activism with headlines that warned, "Protest in the Ranks! The Military's New Dilemma," and "Antiwar G.I.'s and Army Head for Clash over Vietnam."[37] Because of the increased publicity, there was a growing public awareness of dissent within the American military, and the GI movement became one of many widely recognized social and political movements that sprang up within the landscape of late-1960s activism.

Continuing his work as a writer, Fred Gardner promoted the GI movement as the leading edge of antiwar activism. In addition to countless newspaper and magazine articles, Gardner published a book, *The Unlawful Concert: An Account of the Presidio Mutiny Case*, detailing the case of twenty-seven military prisoners who faced courts-martial for a sit-down protest against the war. In 1969, Gardner's notoriety as a writer on radical politics and counterculture caught the attention of Hollywood producers who recruited him to cowrite the screenplay for a new film by renowned Italian director Michelangelo Antonioni. The film, *Zabriskie Point*, turned out to be one of the more memorable cinematic disasters of the era, but the experience allowed Gardner to make connections with a number of influential individuals. One of these was actress Jane Fonda, who approached Gardner at a San Francisco party for the film in early 1970.

Fonda was in the midst of a very public transformation from apolitical celebrity to outspoken antiwar radical and was particularly interested in becoming more involved in the GI movement. While living in Paris in the mid-1960s, she had met American GI activists and members of their civilian support network and returned to the United States in 1969 with a desire to become more directly involved in organizing GIs: "[I had] a commitment to ending the war, and I sensed that working with antiwar soldiers was the best way I could do that. The movement of antiwar soldiers and returned Vietnam veterans was potent, because these men and women were from America's heartland. They had enlisted as patriots; they returned as patriots. They had been there, and this made them more believable to Middle Americans than other groups in the antiwar movement. It was GI resisters, after all, who had brought me into the antiwar movement. I became even more committed to making these new heroes, the new warriors, the focus of my efforts."[38] At the party for *Zabriskie Point*, Fonda asked Gardner about the coffeehouse network he had founded. Gardner promised to send her a map of all the network's locations. She left the party determined to visit the GI coffeehouses herself.[39]

Jane Fonda arrived at the Oleo Strut coffeehouse on the morning of May 11, 1970. After speaking with several GI organizers and civilian staff members,

Fonda gathered a stack of *Fatigue Press* papers and some antiriot control pamphlets and drove to the gates of Fort Hood. She began handing out the material to stunned GIs, who immediately recognized her as the actress perhaps best known for starring in 1968's campy sci-fi sex comedy *Barbarella* (as well as for being the daughter of actor Henry Fonda). Fonda's visit to Fort Hood, one of her first public political actions, was intended to challenge the army regulations she had heard about at the coffeehouse. In that sense, Fonda got exactly what she wanted when military police lieutenant John T. Hoffman approached her and told her that she was under arrest for breaking post regulations. After taking her by car to a Fort Hood police office, Hoffman gave Fonda a letter warning her that if she returned to the base, she would face six months' imprisonment. Upon her release later that afternoon, Fonda immediately returned to the Oleo Strut coffeehouse, where a number of journalists and media figures had assembled, having caught word of a celebrity's presence in town.[40]

The Oleo Strut became the setting for an informal press conference that afternoon, as reporters questioned Fonda about her intentions at Fort Hood. Speaking with clarity and confidence, Fonda proved an articulate spokesperson for the basic goals of the GI movement, declaring, "I'm not here as a movie star—as a publicity stunt. I am a person who is fighting against the war and for GI rights. I went on Fort Hood because GIs aren't allowed to distribute literature there. I think it's appalling that men who are sent overseas to fight and die for their country are denied the constitutional rights which they are supposed to be defending."[41] Photographs of Fonda sitting with Dave Cline and other Oleo Strut staff appeared in both underground and mainstream newspapers. The story of her coffeehouse visit and subsequent arrest helped introduce the GI movement's ideas to a larger section of the American public than ever before.[42]

"THE WHOLE FUCKING TOWN SHUT DOWN": ARMED FARCES DAY(S) IN KILLEEN

At the time of Fonda's visit, GI activists and their civilian supporters were mobilizing for a series of nationally coordinated antiwar demonstrations near military bases around the country. Organizers had chosen the date of May 16, the military's Armed Forces Day, to mark their day of protest.[43] Armed Forces Day was a traditionally sacred day in Killeen, when citizens publicly expressed their patriotism and support for Fort Hood and the American military in general. Killeen's business community made a particular effort to come out strongly on Armed Forces Day, sponsoring local parades and other events to mark their appreciation for the military's presence in Killeen. Activists at the Oleo Strut, however, viewed the day as a chance to express organized opposition to the war. Leaflets and articles in GI newspapers promoted the march as "Armed *Farces* Day." Demonstrating resistance was particularly urgent, according to the event promoters, in the wake of President Nixon's bombing of Cambodia and the shooting of students at Kent State just days earlier.[44]

The 1970 Armed Farces Day march ended up being a much larger event than its organizers anticipated. Several hundred GIs, many in uniform, assembled at the Oleo Strut before marching fifteen blocks (almost the entire length of the town) to a rally at nearby Condor Park. A significant number of counterdemonstrators waved American flags and jeered the parade until Killeen police intervened to separate the groups. At the rally, speakers included veteran Dave Cline, who talked about the spiritual and political transformation he had experienced after killing a young Vietnamese soldier at close range. A group of black soldiers spoke of racism at Fort Hood and their efforts to organize resistance, and Oleo Strut staff members promoted the coffeehouse as the support center for the growing antiwar movement in Killeen.

As Cline later recalled, the unusually large demonstration shocked the Killeen community, which had been relatively insulated from the radical political activism of the era: "The day of the march, all the stores in Killeen closed up and boarded up their windows because they thought there was going to be a riot. The whole fucking town shut down. I'd never seen a whole military town shut down. It was unbelievable."[45] Local media accounts estimated that more than 1,000 GIs and other activists were in the streets of Killeen for the Armed Farces Day event.[46] Despite reports that the majority of the demonstrators were radical civilians "from out of town," photographs from the event, published in the local newspaper, show large numbers of uniformed GIs raising fists, carrying antiwar placards, and flashing peace signs.[47]

On a national level, the 1970 Armed Farces Day event was a tremendous success for its organizers and a significant embarrassment for the military. In anticipation of the day, authorities at more than forty military installations canceled their official celebrations.[48] Staff members at the Oleo Strut were excited about the local possibilities suggested by the surprisingly massive turnout for the parade. As *Fatigue Press* proudly reported, "Everyone understood that May 16 was the first time GIs at Fort Hood had stood together and that a process had been set in motion which could well prove to be unstoppable."[49]

In the months after the Armed Farces Day parade, the Oleo Strut staff worked to expand the kinds of political support and services they could offer to Fort Hood GIs. The goal was to transform the space into a resource center that could serve a wide variety of GI needs, a "kind of living, vibrant, organizational source."[50] The most visible component of this expansion was the opening of a military counseling office in the building's upstairs office space, which was rented with a grant from the Civil Liberties Legal Defense Fund, an organization then raising money for GI movement projects. David Zeiger, a civilian coffeehouse organizer, spent a month in Los Angeles taking a counseling course offered by Ken Cloke, an attorney active in antiwar and civil liberties causes, and returned to Killeen in January 1971 to head the Oleo Strut's legal support campaign. Zeiger helped produce a pamphlet, *GI Legal Self Defense*, that aimed to provide a straightforward summary of a soldier's rights within military law. The pamphlet's wide distribution on post helped promote the Oleo Strut's new legal counseling center, which quickly became a focus of political activity at the coffeehouse.[51]

The counseling center offered three major services: assistance with discharges and applications for conscientious objector status; general education on GI rights, filing harassment complaints, and military law; and direct legal aid for specific cases. A group of Fort Hood GIs began to regularly visit the Oleo Strut counseling office soon after it opened, inquiring about their legal options against a particularly antagonistic commanding officer who had torn a soldier's antiwar posters from his personal locker. Together with activists at the Oleo Strut, the group formed the Spring Offensive Committee (GI-SOC) to organize actions protesting conditions at Fort Hood. In April 1971, GI-SOC circulated a series of petitions that resulted in official investigations and the transfer of several commanding officers. Just a few months into the Oleo Strut's expansion efforts, and in part due to the coffeehouse's increased focus on legal counseling and education, activist soldiers at Fort Hood began making substantive progress in their campaign to address harassment and racism on base.[52]

The spring and summer of 1971 were, as one organizer characterized it, the "heyday" of the Oleo Strut, when the political and cultural energy activists had hoped to create was at a peak. GI-SOC, made up of at least twenty Fort Hood soldiers, met regularly at the coffeehouse to discuss plans for continued actions. As May approached, the group coalesced around the idea of a "second annual" Armed Farces Day parade, building on the success of the previous year's demonstration. GI-SOC structured the parade and rally as the kickoff for an ongoing program of activism and events at Fort Hood and in the larger GI movement. In keeping with the Oleo Strut's new mission to become a "vibrant organizational source," GI-SOC attempted to transform the Armed Farces Day event from an isolated demonstration to the beginning of a more advanced political movement.[53]

The Armed Farces Day event that took place in Killeen, Texas, on May 15, 1971, turned out to be the largest public demonstration in the city's history.[54] David Zeiger happily reported that it was "the most spirited day in the history of the GI movement at Fort Hood."[55] After parading through Killeen, marchers assembled at Condor Park to hear guest speakers and a performance from folk singer Pete Seeger. The day was not without tension. Roughly 200 city police, in riot gear, surrounded the marchers at all times. When one of the guest speakers, a GI from Fort Hood, referred to the police as "motherfuckers," he was pulled from the stage and handcuffed. The large crowd immediately began loudly chanting "Motherfuckers!" in unison, prompting the police to release the soldier, who remounted the stage to triumphant cheers. Even if it took the form of screamed obscenities, the energy at the second annual 1971 Armed Farces Day event in Killeen reflected the GI movement's growing local momentum.

CONFRONTING ECONOMIC EXPLOITATION: THE TYRRELL'S JEWELRY STORE BOYCOTT

Riding high on the success of the 1971 Armed Farces Day event in Killeen, the Spring Offensive Committee decided to direct its political energy toward some of the city's local stores, hoping to stop the predatory sales practices of a number of downtown businesses that depended on GIs for their customer base. To antiwar organizers, the most egregious offender was Tyrrell's Jewelry, part of a national chain of jewelry stores that had cut out a niche in military towns throughout the American South and Midwest. According to a pamphlet handed out at the rally, Tyrrell's business depended on the exploitation of a vulnerable population: "Their philosophy is simple: GIs are there for the taking. Their practice is less simple: it involves psychological warfare playing on guilt, homesickness, love of family, fear of death, and other exploitable emotions shared by most servicemen who are away from home and possibly headed for overseas assignment. Tyrrell's is one of the most vicious examples of the base town business community: people whose livelihood rests on the exploitation and fleecing of GIs who are trapped in that community."[56] GIs at the Oleo Strut were particularly offended by the store's macabre "Vietnam Honor Roll" program, which offered to place a soldier's name on the store's wall if he happened to be killed in Vietnam; the store would also cover any remaining payments owed by the dead soldier. Dave Cline explained that the "Honor Roll" used the war in Vietnam as a sales strategy—an "outrageous" business practice that "tugged on a lonely GI's heartstrings" to sell jewelry.[57] A boycott, the organizers hoped, would draw attention to the economic exploitation of soldiers by Tyrrell's and other local businesses.

In the weeks following the 1971 Armed Farces Day event, large crowds of GIs assembled at the Oleo Strut's GI-SOC meetings. GIs began standing outside the jewelry store on a daily basis, handing out leaflets that detailed Tyrrell's sales tactics and discouraged GIs from entering the shop. In the first weeks of summer, the crowd of GIs and organizers outside Tyrrell's grew, the leafleting turned to picketing, and few, if any, customers walked through the shop's doors.[58] The management at Tyrrell's, understandably concerned for the health of the business, regularly called city police, who on several occasions cited picketers for disturbing the peace. Other local business owners came out in support of Tyrrell's. Ted Connell, owner of Killeen's Connell Chevrolet auto dealership, showed up at the Oleo Strut one evening after he had witnessed activists picketing the jewelry store earlier in the day. He called police from the coffeehouse to make a noise complaint, his local prominence no doubt contributing to the subsequent arrest of a Strut staff member. Tensions between police and picketers escalated over the following days until police finally arrested eight GIs and two civilians for "aiding and abetting an illegal secondary boycott" and "parading without a permit." The ten were held in jail for three days on $2,500 bail until Cam Cunningham, an attorney who represented the Strut and several local GI activists, was able to lower their bail and win their release three days later.[59]

The coalition of activists at the Oleo Strut, with the assistance of Cunningham, filed a suit in federal court demanding that all charges be dropped and that Killeen's "secondary boycott" law be declared unconstitutional.[60] News of the organizers' arrests and the ensuing federal lawsuit spread through both the underground and mainstream media, and by June 1971 Tyrrell's Jewelry stores were being boycotted, picketed, and generally maligned by GIs at military bases around the country. In Killeen, GI activists again assembled outside the store on June 30, an army payday and the beginning of a three-day weekend—prime selling time for Tyrrell's. As the demonstrators assembled, though, the store's managers removed all the jewelry, locked the doors, and placed a sign in the window indicating that the store would be closed for the weekend. The following week, representatives from Tyrrell's corporate office came to the Oleo Strut coffeehouse to negotiate an end to the (now national) GI boycott of their stores. While no formal agreement was reached, Tyrrell's ended its "Vietnam Honor Roll" program at all locations and promised to develop a more "respectful" sales approach. The company's concession to the demands of a relatively small group of GI and civilian activists operating out of a counterculture coffeehouse was a major victory for GI and civilian activists at Fort Hood.[61]

"WE WERE ALL OVER THAT BASE": THE FORT HOOD UNITED FRONT

The Tyrrell's boycott helped sustain the energy created at Killeen's Armed Farces Day event and led directly to the formation of a permanent GI activist group stationed at the Oleo Strut. Beginning in 1971, the Fort Hood United Front became the dominant force in Killeen's GI movement, organizing rallies, distributing petitions, and providing legal advice, all out of the Oleo Strut's expanded upstairs office. In the summer of 1971 the group focused much of its activity on a campaign that sought to win the release of Fort Hood GIs Kelvin Harvey and John Priest. The privates were being held in the stockade on charges stemming from a prison insurrection more than six months earlier; the Fort Hood United Front argued that the soldiers were struggling against the notoriously harsh conditions and overt racism of the Fort Hood stockade and that their prosecution was an attempt to squash their protest.[62] The case was particularly important to the group because of its racial dynamics; Harvey was black and Priest was white. More than 1,000 soldiers signed a petition circulated on base by United Front members, and flyers promoted a "Free Harvey and Priest" gathering and picnic at Killeen's Stillhouse Lake on September 12, 1971.[63]

Nearly 100 GIs came to the Stillhouse Lake event, which was watched closely by military authorities and local police. At the conclusion of the picnic, GIs and other activists piled into a group of cars and headed back to the Oleo Strut. On the way, police pulled over the entire caravan and arrested thirty picnic attendees for disorderly conduct and other charges. The mass arrest resulted in even more negative publicity for police and military authorities, and three days later all charges against Harvey and Priest were dropped.

The pair's military-appointed lawyer, who was in close contact with the United Front and the Oleo Strut staff, later told the activists that the army had backed off of prosecution because they "didn't want to deal" with the Fort Hood United Front.[64]

As the Fort Hood United Front gained a reputation for addressing a wide set of GI issues, a larger number of black soldiers began participating in antiwar activities at the Oleo Strut. One of these soldiers was Private Wes Williams, a Black Panther from Oakland, California, who had been drafted and stationed at Fort Hood in January 1971. Williams first came to the coffeehouse for a screening of a film about Bobby Seale and became involved with the United Front as a way to address the racism that permeated Fort Hood. After Williams organized a particularly successful black-white antiwar rally on October 25, 1971, he and other United Front members were contacted by the office of Representative Ron Dellums (D-Calif.), a member of the Congressional Black Caucus, then conducting an official investigation of racism in the armed forces. Dellums's office informed the activists that another representative, Louis Stokes of Cleveland, would soon visit Fort Hood to hold congressional hearings and that the United Front should gather a group of soldiers who might be willing to testify.[65]

Williams embarked on his mission with energy and efficiency. He personally walked through the Fort Hood barracks, visiting with hundreds of soldiers in the weeks leading up to the hearings, urging them to testify about post conditions. With the assistance of United Front members in companies throughout the post, Williams directed the distribution of more than 2,000 leaflets over the course of a few days, spreading word to GIs of the rare opportunity to express their grievances directly to the federal government. The army itself made no effort to publicize the congressman's visit, and authorities initially insisted on private testimony until GIs demanded and won (with Representative Stokes's support) a public hearing on post.[66]

During Stokes's visit in November 1971, about 200 black soldiers volunteered to testify about racial conditions at Fort Hood. GIs Wes Williams and Bob Paucher (an Oleo Strut staff member) served as Stokes's unofficial post guides, even leading the congressman through an impromptu tour of the prison stockade against the wishes of military authorities, who were struggling to keep up appearances. For two days, the atmosphere at Fort Hood became charged with revolutionary energy. One activist described Fort Hood as "liberated territory—you could do or say anything on the base while the hearings were going on. We were all over that base."⁶⁷ Political discussions, particularly among black GIs, were held openly in barracks while the hearings progressed. One report of the congressman's visit described the feelings of anger and tension among black GIs:

> Brother after Brother testified about the racism that is part of everyday life on Ft. Hood. The fact that blacks are given infantry and artillery jobs; the fact that blacks are prosecuted for 5 minutes AWOL; the fact that blacks are thrown into the stockade arbitrarily and with little reason. Anger was high during the hearing, showing the extent and depth of racism on Ft. Hood, the military, and American society as a whole. A number of times Stokes was asked just what he was going to do with the information gathered. "Since racism is necessary to the military, what are you planning to do to combat it?" one Brother asked. "Are you just here to bullshit for awhile, to pacify us and go back and tell your boss what's happening?"⁶⁸

The meeting revealed that many black GIs at Fort Hood shared the conclusion that Representative Stokes, and the federal government in general, could provide "no immediate relief" for the persistent racial problems on base. On the evening the congressman left Killeen, Wes Williams led a raucous meeting of black soldiers at the Oleo Strut, which was used as a safe discussion space despite many black GIs having reservations about the coffeehouse's reputation as a primarily white hangout. Out of this meeting, a separate black GI organization, the People's Justice Committee, was formed. While standing in front of a mixed crowd of white and black GIs at the Oleo Strut, Williams explained the need for a black-only organization while stressing that the new committee would work closely with both the coffeehouse and the Fort Hood United Front to maintain consistent pressure on military authorities to address the policies that concerned both black and white soldiers on the base.⁶⁹

Shortly after the formation of the People's Justice Committee, Williams was approached by a post commander, General George Seneff, who wanted him to lead a "racial harmony team" as part of the military's renewed efforts to address racial issues on post. Williams refused and shortly thereafter was handed court-martial papers by military police for possession of marijuana. The People's Justice Committee launched an extensive leafleting and petition campaign that helped lead to Williams's acquittal and quiet discharge several weeks later.⁷⁰ The army's quick dismissal of one of the post's most effective and charismatic political organizers was another signal that, at Fort Hood, the GI movement was triggering alarm among military officials.

"THERE WAS A TREMENDOUS RESENTMENT OF THE WAR ON BASE": A YEAR OF CONFRONTATION IN TACOMA

At the same moment that Killeen, Texas, was experiencing an explosion of political activity centered in and around the Oleo Strut coffeehouse, Tacoma, Washington, witnessed a similar phenomenon bursting out of the Shelter Half coffeehouse. The GI-Civilian Alliance for Peace (GI-CAP), until 1969 a small local organization, grew exponentially in public visibility when the Shelter Half came to Tacoma. The coffeehouse offered a place where GI-CAP could do political work; the organization unquestionably benefited from use of the Shelter Half's facilities. Through the winter of 1968–69, GI-CAP meetings packed the coffeehouse, as active-duty soldiers worked alongside local activists to plan a large antiwar demonstration in downtown Seattle for February.[71]

The scale of the GI-CAP-sponsored antiwar demonstration on February 16, 1969, surprised even its organizers. Led by about 300 GIs, nearly 1,000 people representing a diverse range of local and national antiwar organizations paraded through Seattle's downtown, gathering at Tacoma's Eagles Auditorium to listen to a series of speakers on military issues. All of the day's speakers reinforced the ideas that the GI movement sought to address issues beyond the Vietnam War and that actions taken by soldiers around the country were aimed at winning rights and improving conditions for all soldiers, regardless of their political orientation. Army veteran and Socialist Workers Party member Andy Stapp described his efforts to organize GIs into an institution modeled on labor unions, the American Servicemen's Union;[72] army veteran and Socialist Workers Party organizer Howard Petrick described working with GIs at Fort Jackson, South Carolina, to win the right to hold meetings on racism and living conditions on base; and labor leader and political activist Sidney Lens, then cochairman of the National Mobilization Committee, addressed the importance of the civilian antiwar movement's support for dissenting American soldiers.[73] The entire event marked a kind of coming-out party for the Pacific Northwest's growing movement of active-duty GIs and veterans against the war and, just as the members of GI-CAP had hoped, reflected the rising political and organizational cooperation between civilians and soldiers.[74]

As radical groups throughout the Seattle-Tacoma area focused their energies on the GI movement, the Shelter Half coffeehouse played an instrumental role. In addition to providing meeting space, the coffeehouse also became a clearinghouse for antiwar information, mainly by allowing free use of its in-house typewriters, mimeograph machines, and other printing equipment. GI-CAP used this equipment to produce hundreds of issues of *Counterpoint* through 1968 and 1969, but GI-CAP was just one organization among many that took advantage of the Shelter Half's facilities and helped it evolve into one of the most active antiwar underground printing presses in the Pacific Northwest region.[75] Within a relatively brief period, the coffeehouse helped produce and distribute six different underground newspapers and countless leaflets, posters, and pamphlets. Several of these newspapers, including *Vietnam GI, Fed Up!* and *Bottom*, gained recognition on military bases around the world, despite their questionable legal status and entirely improvised underground system of distribution. These newspapers were often smuggled onto bases by GIs willing to risk serious repercussions in order to disseminate alternative viewpoints on the Vietnam War and other military issues.[76]

The civilian wing of the GI movement often saw itself as an independent news service, waging a kind of information war with military authorities. At Fort Lewis, this effort largely took the form of leafleting outside the post's gates, along with the production and distribution of antiwar GI newspapers. In the summer of 1969, however, as a diverse collection of antiwar groups coalesced in and around the Shelter Half coffeehouse, civilian activists (along with a number of active-duty GIs) hatched a plan to dramatically alert the larger Tacoma community about the growing GI movement. The resulting spectacle, dubbed "The Aquatic Invasion of Fort Lewis," ended up being one of the more bizarre antiwar demonstrations of the Vietnam era.

Though the "invasion" included members of GI-CAP, the Socialist Workers Party, the Young Socialist Alliance, and the University of Washington's chapter of Students for a Democratic Society, its main organizer was UW-Seattle student and Young Socialist Alliance member Stephanie Coontz. Beginning in 1967, Coontz established a reputation as one of the campus's most vocal and charismatic antiwar activists. Before the Shelter Half coffeehouse became the center of the Tacoma antiwar movement's efforts to join forces with GIs at Fort Lewis, Coontz and other UW students had been prodding local antiwar activists to more directly engage with the GI movement. The major result of these efforts was the formation of GI-CAP in the fall of 1968, but in the months prior Coontz had been involved in a series of draft resistance and military counseling actions aimed at the college's Reserve Officers' Training Corps program. Coontz was a regular at the Shelter Half coffeehouse during its first year in Tacoma.

At the Shelter Half, Coontz discovered that the relationships she forged with antiwar GIs could help bridge the wide gaps in class, culture, and politics that existed between active-duty GIs and radical college students. According to Coontz, even though the Vietnam War was wildly unpopular at Fort Lewis, the majority of GIs did not, for a variety of reasons, identify with antiwar college students:

> There was a tremendous resentment of the war on base. Inchoate in many ways, not sure who to resent. The rich white kids who didn't have to go, who they saw as yelling at them? Or, the army brass who they hated no matter what their politics were? A lot of it was trying to find common ground to talk to them to make it clear you weren't the press caricature of someone who thinks they're bad guys. . . . You had to move very quickly into a discussion of "We believe that the best way to support our boys is to bring them home. We believe that the people who tell you they support you and then want to leave you there in a war you didn't start, those are not people who support you." And that was so obvious to a lot of GIs, [once] you'd get these conversations started.[77]

At meetings in the coffeehouse, Coontz developed the idea for a grand public gesture demonstrating the civilian antiwar movement's support for disaffected GIs at Fort Lewis. The plan was to stage a "mock invasion" of the base, using guerrilla theater to ridicule military authority and promote solidarity with young soldiers. The tongue-in-cheek spectacle, which took place in July 1969, was designed to coincide with the Nixon administration's media campaign promoting American withdrawal from Vietnam, a campaign that had used Fort Lewis GIs as evidence of de-escalation. By scheduling its own publicity stunt in Tacoma on the weekend immediately following the official "Welcome Home" parade in Seattle, Coontz and other antiwar activists intended to subvert the administration's public celebration of "peace with honor" and lampoon the government's own propaganda efforts.[78]

While planning the Aquatic Invasion stunt, Coontz made sure that a number of press outlets would cover the mock invasion. She shared her plans with Don McGavin, a television reporter for Seattle's local NBC affiliate, KOMO, who agreed to send a camera crew.[79] On July 13, 1969, a group of fifty civilians met on the public side of American Lake in Tacoma, a body of water that shared its shores with the heavily guarded Fort Lewis property. Coontz, wearing a military uniform and sunglasses, led a flotilla of small inflatable rafts, most of them emblazoned with the GI movement's well-known "FTA" sign. Upon reaching the Fort Lewis side of American Lake, the boats were halted by several confused MPs, who announced, to no one's shock, that the group would not be allowed access to the base. Coontz and her cohorts assembled on the small beach, handing out leaflets to a group of GIs as Coontz delivered a tongue-in-cheek "victory speech." The scene culminated when a "frogman" emerged from the water in a peace-sign-decorated Navy SEAL wetsuit and dragged a round "negotiation table" onto the sand. After being held for a brief period, all of the activists were released by military authorities.[80] Coontz's statement, and the leaflets handed out on base, parodied the U.S. government's own notorious statements on Vietnam. "If we don't fight them on the shores of Ft. Lewis," Coontz declared, "we will have to fight them on the shores of American Lake. Our honor is at stake. We must bring freedom to the peace-loving EMs at Fort Lewis. And if it becomes necessary to destroy Ft. Lewis in order to save it, we shall not shrink from that task."[81] The leaflets concluded by speaking directly to GIs, underlining the invasion stunt's higher purpose: "You all know this invasion is a joke. But your Constitutional rights are not a joke."[82]

A few months after the Aquatic Invasion stunt, in October 1969, the first issues of an antiwar GI newspaper, *Fed Up!*, were printed at the Shelter Half and distributed on base. The newspaper's opening editorial put its radical politics up front: "*Fed Up!* is written and edited by a group of Fort Lewis GIs who can no longer stand the oppression of the US military services. Not just the oppression we all feel as members of the military, but the oppression the US uses to try to control the people of Nam, Korea, Latin America, and the United States. We're also sick and tired of the lies and half truths the military uses to support their imperialistic actions both abroad and at home. That's why we decided to get together and print the truth."[83] Though the content found on the pages of *Fed Up!* was created entirely by GIs, it was produced with the printing facilities and civilian staff of the Shelter Half, who ensured that more than 5,000 copies of the paper's inaugural issue made their way to the base.[84] In its first months of publication, *Fed Up!* became popular at Fort Lewis and on bases around the country.

On October 20, 1969, a group of nearly fifty GIs, and several civilians, gathered in the Cascadian Service Club room at Post 35 on the grounds of Fort Lewis. The group discussed the formation of a local American Servicemen's Union chapter, with union founder Andy Stapp present along with a number of civilian organizers. During the meeting, military police burst into the room and arrested thirty-five soldiers and three civilians, including Stapp. The men were detained for "conducting an unauthorized meeting of a political nature on the post."[85] Although ultimately released, according to organizers at the Shelter Half, many of the soldiers present at the meeting endured subsequent recrimination and harassment, including shipment to Vietnam.[86] Seventeen of these soldiers filed a suit in federal court on October 29 "asking the court to guarantee their rights of free speech and assembly under the First Amendment."[87] Stapp and the other civilian organizers filed a similar suit, backed by the Seattle branch of the American Civil Liberties Union. Fort Lewis's GI activism again became a focus of national media attention.[88]

In December 1969, after receiving free legal counsel at the Shelter Half coffeehouse, six Fort Lewis GIs filed for conscientious objector status, effectively refusing their orders for service in Vietnam.[89] After this unprecedented incident of resistance, combined with the previous months of rising insubordination, the army took an extraordinary step, intervening directly on the operation of the coffeehouse. In a letter dated December 11, 1969, addressed to the "Proprietor" of the Shelter Half, U.S. Navy captain H. W. Stauffacher—the president of the Armed Forces Disciplinary Control Board, Western Washington-Oregon Area—notified the coffeehouse that he had initiated action to place it "OFF LIMITS" for all military personnel. "The board took this action after receiving information that the Shelter Half is a source of dissident counseling and literature and other activities inimical to the good morale, order and discipline within the Armed Services," Stauffacher stated, adding that the coffeehouse would have an opportunity to defend itself at a hearing scheduled for January 22, 1970.[90] The disciplinary board's action against the Shelter Half revealed that government authorities had recognized the obvious: interactions between antiwar civilians and GIs at off-base coffeehouses were contributing to a dramatic acceleration of antiwar political activity in the army. As would soon become clear, U.S. military and government officials were only beginning to coordinate a response.

[3]

Repression, Harassment, Intimidation

Crushing the Coffeehouses

> The coffeehouse is an undeniable threat to the military hierarchy because GIs there have the chance to think, to understand how the military is using them to maintain their power over little people around the world and nation. The coffeehouse is a threat to local authority because the army controls jobs for their community and money for their pockets.
>
> *Fun Travel Adventure*, no. 17 (May 1970)

CONGRESS INVESTIGATES THE COFFEEHOUSE NETWORK

GI coffeehouses created intense concern among military leaders and government officials from the moment they began to appear in and around American military towns. Over the course of the coffeehouse network's existence, its leaders and support organizations were subjected to intense scrutiny from the federal government, which hoped to neutralize the antiwar movement's growing influence among active-duty GIs. In responding to the GI coffeehouse phenomenon, though, political and military leaders often found themselves in disagreement over both the origins of the network itself and, more important, how best to deal with it.

The first wave of federal attention came from the coffeehouse network's association with the National Mobilization Committee to End the War in Vietnam ("Mobe"), after the antiwar group's prominent role in demonstrations at the Democratic Party's national convention in Chicago in August 1968. Rennie Davis and Tom Hayden, along with several other Mobe leaders and political activists collectively dubbed "the Chicago Eight," were eventually indicted and tried in federal court for conspiracy, resulting in one of the more memorable public trials of the 1960s protest era. In the months before this indictment, the House Un-American Activities Committee (HUAC) held a series of hearings to investigate "subversive involvement in the disruption of the 1968 Democratic Party National Convention."[1]

In December 1968, Davis and Hayden testified before HUAC. During their respective interrogations, congressional committee members showed an intense interest in the GI coffeehouse phenomenon and the civilian antiwar movement's efforts to support military dissent.[2] Although both Davis and Hayden repeatedly explained, in their testimony before HUAC, that the coffeehouses were designed to support an antiwar movement *already in progress* within the army, the committee members refused to acknowledge the possibility of dissent emerging from the ranks of GIs, insisting that "outside agitators" were behind any discontent expressed by soldiers. When Davis was specifically asked if his goal was to "encourage disaffection and desertion from the Army," he denied the charges, explaining that the coffeehouse network's purpose was not to indoctrinate soldiers but rather to develop an alternative cultural space for young people in the military:

> We do not urge any young soldier to take any action that would put him in legal jeopardy with the United States military, nor do we in any of our coffeehouses counsel young men to desert. Our purpose is to try to provide a place for the young man who has given his body to Uncle Sam so that he does not have to give his mind. Our place is to provide rest and relaxation for basic trainees who around the fifth week of their basic training learn to kill. He has something to escape to, other than the whorehouses and saloons that make up these small towns, like in Waynesville or Killeen, Texas, where there are people who generally care about him and are not trying to extract or steal his body for prostitution purposes. There are people who want to keep his mind alive, and not be totally sold out to the military machine. There are people there who essentially say, "I am from the peace movement because I care about the hell you are going through." That is the essential idea of the coffeehouse—pretty good.[3]

Throughout their testimony, Davis and Hayden repeatedly made connections between youth culture and antiwar politics, portraying the coffeehouse network as a hybrid project that hoped to employ the aesthetics and orientation of youth culture for specific political purposes. As Davis put it, GI coffeehouses were primarily cultural institutions, places "where we can hopefully bring good entertainment, and kind of provide an antidote to the virus of the USO."[4]

In his own HUAC appearance, Tom Hayden similarly stressed the central role that youth culture played in undermining the authority of institutions ranging from the Chicago police force to HUAC itself. Hayden rather smugly declared that, despite the committee's illusions of power, the young people of America had already won on the battleground of culture: "Politicians of the kind like Dean Rusk, Lyndon Johnson, Richard Nixon, Hubert Humphrey, these people are in a sense already finished, because they can't exercise any authority; they have no respect from wide sections of the American people. Richard Nixon does not even believe that Beatles' albums should be played. He believes that drugs are the curse of American youth." Hayden's easy transition between political figures like Nixon and rock bands like the Beatles reflected the widely held notion, in antiwar circles, that youth culture's popularity foretold permanent changes in the American political landscape and, specifically, in the ability of the U.S. Army to fill its ranks with willing young draftees.[5]

HUAC members were not impressed. As Davis's testimony concluded, Representative Albert Watson angrily interrupted him to declare, "You have nothing but contempt for this committee, for the President, Secretary Rusk, and everything else!"[6] To Watson and other committee members, coffeehouses were part of a sinister conspiracy, hatched by the same dangerous radicals who had allegedly incited riots in Chicago, to indoctrinate loyal GIs. HUAC members refused to believe that American soldiers might organize political activity on their own. And no amount of evidence could convince them otherwise.

Three years after HUAC's initial investigation into GI coffeehouses, government concern about a perceived crisis in the U.S. military came to a peak. Colonel Robert L. Heinl, a retired Marine colonel and frequent contributor to military publications, helped fan the flames of institutional alarm when his widely read and influential article "The Collapse of the Armed Forces" was published in *Armed Forces Journal* in June 1971.[7] Heinl documented a series of disturbing phenomena, including increased incidents of racial violence, drug abuse, "fraggings" (murder of superior officers), political activism, desertion, and general insubordination. The article's near-hysterical tone and sensational claims (Heinl characterized rebellious black soldiers as "headhunters" out for white blood) set off a flurry of media attention in the months following its publication. The piece even garnered an official reaction from the Department of Defense, which conceded "problems" but downplayed Heinl's often pessimistic conclusions.[8]

Responding to Heinl's article and the resulting media fallout, in October 1971 the renamed Committee on Internal Security[9] initiated an investigation of "civilian subversion" of the U.S. military. The committee chair, Representative Richard Ichord (D-Mo.), opened the proceedings by reading a statement titled "Contributing Factors to the Morale Crisis in the Armed Services," cataloging the many distressing symptoms of the now widely recognized crisis in the armed forces. Ichord acknowledged that the unpopularity of the war in Vietnam had taken a dramatic toll on military morale but insisted that the war alone was not enough to explain the nearly mutinous situation described by Heinl and other observers. As was perhaps predictable, Ichord suggested that dark forces on the Left were in fact responsible: "One aspect of this morale situation which has not been widely revealed or understood is the matter of attempted subversion of the men in uniform by militant extremists of the far left. These include, of course, those with Marxist-Leninist leanings who actually seek a Communist victory in Asia and hope to promote an American defeat or, at least, a humiliation of this country and its military forces."[10]

Ichord's statement included a specific definition of the GI movement that suggests the committee's almost willful misunderstanding of the larger political and cultural context that contributed to its existence: "The 'GI Movement' is the term used by the radical left to refer to that aspect of the antiwar movement directed against the military.... The available facts indicate that the GI movement exists primarily outside the military and is essentially a civilian movement."[11] Ignoring the thousands of young soldiers who participated in one form or another, choosing instead to see the GI movement as the product of outside agitation by enemies of the state, Ichord and the rest of the committee imagined an exaggerated scenario that reduced a complex phenomenon to an anticommunist talking point.

During its five-day investigation, the committee was chiefly concerned with the GI coffeehouse network, identifying it as the most obvious base of operations for the radical Left's plans to infiltrate the armed services. Heinl's article, the source of so many of the committee's allegations, had explicitly characterized the coffeehouses in this manner, referring to them as institutions that "ply GI's with rock music, lukewarm coffee, antiwar literature, how-to-do-it tips on desertion, and similar disruptive counsels" and asserting that most of these coffeehouses were in fact sponsored by "a communist front organization."[12] If radical outsiders were responsible for the problems in the military, the committee assumed, the nation's growing network of GI coffeehouses would be the place to root them out.

In its final report, spanning more than 1,200 pages, the committee collected testimony transcripts, visual materials, clippings from the underground GI press, and dozens of photographs depicting GI coffeehouses, mug shots of GI organizers, and surveillance photos of various GI movement events. Despite the massive scope of the investigation, however, the committee's report contained few substantive conclusions about the nature of the GI movement and its possible relationship to the military's well-publicized morale problem. Committee members seemed curiously obsessed with Marxism, in one case asking a witness nearly a dozen detailed questions about the types of books she found on a coffeehouse shelf. As the committee itself admitted in its final report, these details did not come close to proving any kind of criminal subversion. That an antiwar coffeehouse would stock Marxist literature on its shelves was simply not as shocking in 1971 as it might have been a decade earlier.[13]

On the last day of its investigation, the committee interviewed several military officials who offered a decidedly different interpretation of the military morale crisis. Rowland A. Morrow, an investigatory director from the Department of Defense, explained that, by the department's own estimations, the actual influence of radical politics on GIs was minimal, despite the committee's assumptions about outside indoctrination. When committee members repeatedly asked why the coffeehouse network had not been more aggressively policed by military and government authorities, Morrow pointed out that GI coffeehouses were public spaces and that visiting one was not, in and of itself, an act of subversion. Committee members were frustrated by the Department of Defense's seeming passivity toward what they considered a treasonous coffeehouse network and expressed their hope that federal action could shut the coffeehouses down.[14]

"FUCK THE ARMY": FIGHTING IT OUT ON THE LOCAL LEVEL

In addition to these congressional investigations, every GI coffeehouse project experienced some form of official or unofficial harassment, intimidation, or investigation throughout the network's existence. As the network's chief source of financial support, the United States Servicemen's Fund spent most of its resources defending the network from these attacks. Costs could range from the relatively small expense of replacing broken windows and smashed stereo equipment at the Oleo Strut in Killeen, Texas, to the considerably larger sums required to defend the owners of the UFO coffeehouse in Columbia, South Carolina, from criminal prosecution in 1970. In the case of the USSF's attempt to open a coffeehouse in Muldraugh, Kentucky, outside Fort Knox, in 1969, for example, the price of responding to harassment became prohibitive to the entire project and provided a stark lesson on the confluence of repressive forces, both public and private, then rising in opposition to the antiwar movement's activity within the military.

At Fort Knox, an antiwar movement had been growing among GIs since July 1968, when four soldiers produced and distributed the first issue of *Fun Travel Adventure* (the "FTA" initials making a sly reference to the ubiquitous GI movement catchphrase "Fuck the Army"). By the summer of 1969, dozens of Fort Knox GIs were meeting with a growing number of civilians at several off-post locations, and as the group became larger, participants recognized the need for a stable meeting place; a GI coffeehouse seemed the logical extension of the GI-civilian alliance forming in Muldraugh and nearby Louisville, Kentucky. On August 30, 1969, the Fort Knox Coffeehouse opened in tiny Muldraugh and was immediately set upon by city authorities. The day after opening, local police raided the coffeehouse and took the names of every person inside. The following day, the city of Muldraugh passed a law requiring new businesses to be subjected to a "detailed police investigation" in order to obtain an operating license. By September 5, the city attorney had convinced the building's landlord to revoke the coffeehouse's lease, and sheriff's deputies officially shuttered the coffeehouse just six days after it opened its doors.[15]

The organizers of the Fort Knox Coffeehouse refused to back down, and the coffeehouse reopened less than a month later after a large rally of GIs and civilians in downtown Muldraugh. Through the entirety of the coffeehouse's tenure in Muldraugh, though, a number of local groups waged a relentless battle to drive its organizers away. Over the final months of 1969 and into 1970, extralegal intimidation, including physical violence, combined with a concerted campaign of police harassment made operation of the coffeehouse virtually impossible. On two separate occasions, unknown parties lobbed firebombs through the coffeehouse windows (there was minimal damage), and both civilian and GI coffeehouse staff were routinely arrested when distributing leaflets and newspapers near the post or in town. In March 1970, a group of antiwar civilians and GIs who had been leafleting in the parking lot of a local burger restaurant were attacked by several men with bats and clubs; after the men stole a camera, beat a civilian organizer, and vandalized the car of a coffeehouse staff member, the police arrived to quell the violence. The men with clubs fled; police arrested the three bloodied GI organizers for disorderly conduct.[16]

The relentless arrests took a substantial toll on the Fort Knox Coffeehouse's financial resources. In the fall of 1969, when six coffeehouse organizers were indicted in city court for "operating a common nuisance where evil and ill disposed people frequent," their bail was set at $1,500 each (the equivalent of nearly $10,000 today). Authorities were surprised when the activists were able to pay the considerable sum, perhaps explaining why city police arrested four additional staff members the following day and collected another set of comparable bonds, further undermining the coffeehouse's chances of survival in Muldraugh. But the unfair treatment seemed to strengthen solidarity among the GIs and civilians who frequented the coffeehouse; when the entire civilian staff was in jail on October 30, 1969, twenty active-duty soldiers risked their own arrests by taking over its operation for the evening.[17]

After the campaign of arrests and intimidation of civilian staff, GIs at Fort Knox took a more dominant role in the coffeehouse's everyday operation and, perhaps more important, in the coordination of antiwar activities in town and on post. Ultimately, though, defending the coffeehouse from harassment drained the resources and morale of GI and civilian antiwar organizers at Fort Knox. By April 1970, the coffeehouse was closed completely, with those civilian organizers not in city jail moving on to work at other GI projects around the country.[18] At Fort Knox, antiwar GIs would continue their activism against the war, most notably by continuing to publish *Fun Travel Adventure*, but without the support of an off-post coffeehouse and its staff of civilian activists.

The repression and harassment of local GI projects was unsurprising to GI organizers and their supporters, who had anticipated intense resistance. But many organizers were still taken aback by the degree of hostility and hatred some of the local GI projects provoked. At the Oleo Strut coffeehouse in Killeen, Texas, the civilian and GI staff, in their reports to national antiwar organizations, repeatedly reported their feelings of isolation and alienation from the Killeen community, whose citizens often expressed open hostility to the coffeehouse's presence. The coffeehouse was a frequent topic of discussion on the *Killeen Daily Herald*'s editorial page, which seemed to delight in printing venomous letters from local citizens voicing animosity toward everything the coffeehouse stood for.

In May 1971, a local minister, Reverend Daniel Deutsch of Trinity Lutheran Church, wrote a letter to the *Herald* to defend the Oleo Strut, arguing that the arrest of ten activists outside the coffeehouse represented an assault on individual liberties: "It is with deep regret that we are now witnessing here in Killeen the repression of individual freedom and expression that is pervading our country. It is tragic that people cannot dress differently, wear their hair differently, or hold and express unpopular views without being harassed and even arrested for simply being different. I would willingly wager a good sum that ten well-dressed, well-groomed businessmen standing in front of a business establishment in the same area would not even have received a passing glance from the arresting officers."[19]

Deutsch's letter created a major stir. For several weeks, the *Herald* printed outraged responses from Killeen citizens who were incensed by Deutsch's support of the Oleo Strut. "If Brother Deutsch will stroll by the Oleo Strut almost any evening, he will hear some of the most obscene language and absolute profanity he will ever hear. He will also see signs displayed that are not very decent, if not absolutely obscene and anti-Godly and anti-American," declared Pastor Don Scott of Northside Baptist Church. Killeen resident Coy W. Hilbert asked, "Is it really an issue of hair and dress? Wouldn't it be more a matter of morals? Does God condone filth, adultery, stealing, slander, willfully breaking laws, etc.? Killeen has been plagued with all of these. . . . Freedom and the rights of good moral people are suffering due to the acts of so-called 'freedom marchers.'"[20] Some writers aimed their anger directly at antiwar GIs themselves, blaming them for disrupting the war effort and hoping that military policy changes would eliminate dissent in the future. As one of these writers, who signed her letter "Mrs. Marion Jones, Army wife, and proud of it," angrily declared, "The whole damned bunch of these soldiers do not rate the privilege of shining the boots of one serious-minded, well-behaved American soldier. The sooner we get an all volunteer Army and can dispose of this garbage, the sooner the whole Army will begin to be respected by the civilian population again."[21]

For their part, the editors of the *Killeen Daily Herald* often took the opportunity to reinforce this contempt for the Oleo Strut, characterizing antiwar and counterculture activities as anomalies in an otherwise loyal, patriotic military town. To the chorus of disapproving citizens, the paper added its own voice: "The sight of police dragging antiwar protestors to the city jail on charges of violating the parade ordinance is a new experience for this military community. . . . The pictures of bearded youths laying on the sidewalks and being dragged to jail by police are a sorry spectacle. We have watched these conflicts in other cities, but it brings special embarrassment when they happen in Killeen, where men in uniform have learned that peace cannot always be won by collapsing on the ground."[22]

The Oleo Strut was not alone in confronting local hostility. In rural Mountain Home, Idaho, where soldiers from nearby Mountain Home Air Force Base began meeting in early 1971 at a converted theater called the Covered Wagon, the public campaign against the coffeehouse seemed to come from every level of the local population. Mark Lane, one of the Covered Wagon's civilian organizers, described the mood in Mountain Home in the months after the coffeehouse opened:

> During the past year, hostility from some quarters toward the Wagon grew so intense that the local newspaper published letters urging physical attacks upon the Wagon and its members. A number of members were subsequently attacked, the doors and windows of the coffeehouse were smashed on 20 different occasions, [and] a member of the City Council, speaking at a council meeting, voiced approval for the attackers, insisting they were "just doing their thing." My own life has been threatened.... One minister prayed at a regular Sunday morning service for God to destroy the Covered Wagon. Not a single church has opened its doors to our members in Mountain Home, and some have literally slammed their doors in the faces of GIs.[23]

In the fall of 1971, the intimidation of the Covered Wagon became even more intense when a group of local men severely beat a patron inside the coffeehouse. Days later, vandals broke into the premises overnight, leaving the words "This is just a warning" spray-painted on the walls. Finally, on November 21, 1971, six months after opening, arsonists burned the Covered Wagon to the ground. The coffeehouse's intentional destruction was never investigated by town authorities.[24]

The Covered Wagon's burning produced an outpouring of support from national antiwar organizations, most notably the USSF, which helped raise funds to rebuild the destroyed theater building. In letters asking for support, which appeared in national newspapers and magazines, the USSF depicted the Covered Wagon as a vital resource for antiwar GIs in the region, highlighting the diverse services offered by the coffeehouse and stressing the importance of civilian support of the GI movement: "The Covered Wagon was an old theater which GIs converted, with many hours of hard work, into a meeting place for their off-base activities. These include publication of their newspaper, *The Helping Hand*, military counseling on GI rights, women's meetings, political education sessions, music groups, and work with local people, such as The Idaho Migrants Program. In short, the project, which offers an alternative to the daily abuses of the military system, used the coffeehouse as its center. . . . We feel the GI Movement must have the support of all people who desire a quick end to the war in Indochina."[25] The USSF's fund-raising campaign helped contribute to the Covered Wagon's reopening in another location just weeks after the theater was burned down, and over the next several years the Mountain Home GI movement made a significant local impact.[26]

Perhaps the most frightening incident of violence in the GI coffeehouse network's history occurred at the Fort Dix Coffeehouse in Wrightstown, New Jersey, in early 1970. On February 8, six men in military uniforms, including a captain and a sergeant first class, entered the coffeehouse and proceeded to "harass the hell out of the GIs," ripping newspapers out of their hands and tossing them on the floor, preventing phone calls from being made, and attempting to provoke fights. After coffeehouse staff evicted them, the men replied, "We will return."[27] One week later, the coffeehouse was celebrating Valentine's Day with a crowd of about thirty GIs and their dates. At approximately 8:45 p.m., the coffeehouse door opened and what appeared to be a metal canister rolled into the center of the floor. Several GIs recognized the canister as a grenade and attempted to throw it out the door. Before they could, though, the grenade exploded, seriously injuring two Fort Dix soldiers, Privates Donald Hutchinson and James Shoenung, and one civilian, nineteen-year-old Mildred Baker.[28] No one was ever arrested for the grenade attack.

In a 1970 *Los Angeles Free Press* interview, Howard Levy of the USSF was asked what he thought civilians could do to support antiwar GIs. He replied, "I think civilians must appreciate the fact that within the past two weeks, the MDM [Movement for a Democratic Military] office in Oceanside, California, had twelve rounds of .45 caliber bullets fired into it. One GI was hurt, but he's doing fine now. Recently, the Fort Dix Coffeehouse in New Jersey was subjected to a hand grenade attack. The coffeehouse at Fort Knox, Kentucky, was firebombed three times." Levy and the USSF wanted to convince civilians that GI activism was an important part of a larger movement for social justice, linking the reactionary violence to which it was subjected to that experienced by other revolutionary groups, such as the Black Panthers in Oakland, California. "There's an enormous amount of repression coming down on the GI movement and the civilians who support that movement," Levy emphasized. "That repression is exceeded only by the repression that's coming down on the Black Panthers. It is therefore of extreme importance that civilians, in any way possible, demonstrate their solidarity, their support for the GI movement."[29] To organizers, the fact that coffeehouses were subjected to violent attacks proved the desperate need for civilian-supported meeting spaces for antiwar soldiers.

While extralegal assaults on coffeehouses were the subject of sensational headlines, it was official harassment, in the form of constant arrests, that proved far more financially taxing for coffeehouse supporters. By a large margin, bail money and legal defense accounted for the most substantial portion of the USSF's budget, as coffeehouse organizers around the country, including GIs, were routinely thrown in jail by local and military police. The arrests were so frequent and carried such high bonds for relatively minor infractions (most often for violations like trespassing, loitering, or being a public nuisance) that many organizers suspected a coordinated effort on the part of local and military authorities to make life nearly impossible for anyone associated with a coffeehouse.[30]

Indeed, as government records reveal, suspicions of a conspiracy were sometimes well founded. Federal authorities had their eyes on the coffeehouse phenomenon from the moment it first appeared in Columbia, South Carolina, and took immediate action to disrupt its effectiveness. At the time, the FBI's counterintelligence program was operating around the country under director J. Edgar Hoover's orders to "expose, disrupt, misdirect, discredit, or otherwise neutralize" subversive political organizations. In July 1968, the director issued to all FBI field offices a letter titled "Disruption of the New Left" that included specific plans for FBI agents to undermine the activities of antiwar groups. Hoover singled out the GI coffeehouse network as a target for special attention: "New Left groups are attempting to open coffeehouses near military bases in order to influence members of the Armed Forces. Wherever these coffeehouses are, friendly news media should be alerted to them and their purpose. In addition, various drugs, such as marijuana, will probably be utilized by individuals running the coffeehouses or frequenting them. Local law enforcement authorities should be promptly advised whenever you receive an indication that this is being done."[31] Federal agents thus became one part of a coordinated effort to harass antiwar activists at coffeehouse locations around the country. Of course, each coffeehouse project had a unique local experience with harassment and intimidation, experiences that ran the gamut from relatively benign (angry letters in the local newspaper) to downright frightening (arrest and imprisonment on felony charges). The common thread through all this harassment, though, was a consistent underlying message: GI coffeehouses and their supporters were not welcome in America's military towns.

"OFF LIMITS": THE SHELTER HALF CATCHES HELL

In January 1970, the Shelter Half coffeehouse in Tacoma, Washington, became the first GI coffeehouse project declared officially "off limits" by military authorities. A critical component of the military's argument for the coffeehouse's restricted status was that its staff members directly counseled soldiers to commit crimes (specifically, going AWOL or otherwise refusing duty). In the weeks leading up to a scheduled hearing on the coffeehouse's restricted status, a number of undercover agents visited the coffeehouse and attempted to engage staff members in various criminal activities, from drug dealing to promoting armed insurrection on base. Well accustomed to these kinds of tactics, the staff eventually held a press conference to emphasize that the coffeehouse did not promote desertion and in fact encouraged disaffected GIs to explore the military's available legal channels.[32]

To the operators of the Shelter Half, the military's aggressive campaign against the coffeehouse was obviously political, intended to blunt the impact of the antiwar movement's efforts to work with soldiers at Fort Lewis. Matthew Rinaldi, a civilian organizer who worked at the Shelter Half during its first two years in town, pointed out to the *Tacoma News Tribune* that the military's "off limits" designation marked a significant change in policy. Historically, the military had deemed businesses to be "off limits" only in the cases of houses of prostitution, homosexual bars, and places of known narcotic activity. By attempting to ban soldiers from going to the Shelter Half, military officials widened their definition of potentially harmful establishments to include politically themed coffeehouses. "The military is blatantly and admittedly moving for political reasons in this case. We consider this a test case because if the government is successful here it could move against the moratoriums and political meetings and the entire anti-war movement," Rinaldi explained, echoing a widely held suspicion among coffeehouse organizers and others in the GI movement that the federal government (specifically, the Nixon White House) was behind the more aggressive administrative attacks against their organizations and members.[33]

In the month leading up to the scheduled "off limits" hearing, organizers at the Shelter Half, along with a number of soldiers from Fort Lewis who regularly visited the coffeehouse, initiated a publicity campaign and demonstrations to call attention to the military's escalating policies. In special issues of locally produced GI newspapers, both GIs and civilians defended the coffeehouse's right to exist and reminded Fort Lewis soldiers that the Shelter Half would remain open to them regardless of the army's designation. GI writers cast the coffeehouse's struggles in the context of the larger GI movement, asserting that the army's campaign against the coffeehouse was part of an effort to silence dissent among soldiers and limit their access to critiques of the war: "The brass are trying to tell us who we can talk with and what we can read. The Shelter Half is one of the links between the GI movement and the civilian movement. They provide material and moral support for our struggle. Now the military wants to keep us from our meeting place. They're afraid of what will happen when we will no longer be used as robots and slaves. But they can't stop us from getting together. The Shelter Half is ours."[34] By threatening to ban soldiers from visiting the coffeehouse, officials at Fort Lewis inadvertently helped call attention, for many soldiers, to the Shelter Half's important role in the local GI movement. The coffeehouse's fight against military authority echoed the local GI movement's own efforts to secure civil liberties for enlisted men.

As the Shelter Half's January 22 hearing approached, its operators continued to mount their publicity campaign to defend the coffeehouse, helping mobilize the Seattle-Tacoma area's robust antiwar community. A group of activist attorneys volunteered their pro bono legal services, and the American Servicemen's Union held regular meetings at the coffeehouse to discuss the defense strategy. In concert with these actions, a large group of students at the University of Washington in Seattle helped organize an on-campus event to publicize the coffeehouse's fight and bring attention to the harassment faced by dissident soldiers. This event, billed as "the Trial of the Army," ended up becoming, for a number of reasons, one of the most successful and important public demonstrations in the history of GI activism.[35]

Held on January 21, 1970 (one day before the originally scheduled military hearing), the mock trial was, at its heart, an act of guerrilla theater, one of the New Left's favorite forms of public satire. The "Trial of the Army" parodied the military's proposed "off limits" order, using the Shelter Half's persecution to point out military hypocrisy. On the stage of the Husky Ballroom at the center of the university campus, a "jury" of thirteen active-duty servicemen listened to testimony from a variety of witnesses who spoke about daily life in the Vietnam War–era U.S. Army, including conditions in prison stockades, racism, harassment, and, of course, the experience of the war itself.[36] Hundreds of civilians, students, and soldiers crowded into the space, raising their fists and chanting revolutionary slogans in response to each of the speakers. The most electrifying moment occurred when an AWOL GI, who had escaped from an armed guard at Fort Lewis a week earlier and was at that moment a fugitive from military justice, took the stage surrounded by ten uniformed GI "bodyguards." His voice shaking, he told the crowd of his terror at being hunted by military police for not wanting to go to Vietnam.[37]

More than fifty local GIs risked punishment and harassment to speak at the Shelter Half–sponsored "Trial of the Army." One of these soldiers, Private Wade Carson, went to extraordinary lengths to participate in the event. In the days leading up to the trial, Carson was arrested on post and held in pretrial confinement after an officer witnessed him handing a single copy of *Fed Up!* to another Fort Lewis GI. Unlike other GIs then being punished for various crimes, Carson was not confined to the stockade but was rather issued an order that he could not leave the post, even during off-duty hours. He was also assigned a personal guard by military officials, who ordered the guard to make sure Carson did not speak to any other soldiers. Despite being held under these conditions, Carson was able to arrange a visit with a Shelter Half attorney, who helped him to covertly record a politically charged statement on audiotape. The tape was played as the first "witness" during the mock trial just days later, Carson's disembodied voice a stark reminder of the treatment often given to political dissidents within the armed forces.[38] Carson's alleged deception in recording the message only added to the ire directed at him from post authorities, who confined him in the stockade after learning of the tape's existence. Though the details of Carson's case were extraordinary, most of the soldiers who participated in the Shelter Half's mock trial reported some form of official or unofficial recrimination in the weeks following the demonstration.[39]

The Shelter Half's "Trial of the Army" marked the apex of a month-long media campaign by coffeehouse organizers and supporters, and the resulting publicity seemed to make an impact on the official army position toward GI coffeehouses. A few days before the planned hearing, the Armed Forces Disciplinary Board delivered a letter to the Shelter Half, reporting that the "off limits" hearing had been "indefinitely postponed." The Shelter Half's seeming victory marked an important moment for the GI coffeehouse movement, as military authorities backed off the aggressive tactics taken toward off-base meeting places, of which the Shelter Half's proposed "off limits" designation was only one example.[40]

Perhaps most important, the Shelter Half's brief experience with official military repression contributed to an outburst of political organizing and demonstrations throughout the Pacific Northwest that reflected the particular strength and diversity of the region's radical communities. The "Trial of the Army" showcased this diverse local presence, as groups representing a wide range of left-oriented interests came together to show support for a threatened institution. In the GI underground press and at the mock trial itself, the coffeehouse's struggle and the challenges faced by the GI movement were explicitly connected to working-class and related liberation movements. At the event, a representative from the United Farm Workers, Dale Van Pelt, spoke at length about the national grape boycott, comparing poor agricultural laborers to the exploited "grunts" of a working-class army and proposing that a union model of labor organization, like that being built by the American Servicemen's Union, could help ameliorate these shared injustices.[41] Another speaker announced the formation of an all-Indian GI organization, Hew-Kekaw-Na-Yo ("to resist"); the group went on to publish a widely read, if briefly produced, GI newspaper called *Yah-Hoh* throughout 1970.[42] *Yah-Hoh* called attention to the specific issues faced by Native American soldiers and contributed to a surge of specialized GI publications covering an expansive set of ethnic, racial, and cultural categories characteristic of the American political landscape in the early 1970s.[43] The Shelter Half's comparatively small battle with military authorities had sparked an intense local reaction that situated and articulated the coffeehouse's predicament as part of a range of critical issues facing American society during the Vietnam War era.

A "CESSPOOL OF EVIL": THE UFO COFFEEHOUSE ON TRIAL

The UFO coffeehouse in Columbia, South Carolina, caught the attention of officials in Washington when the Fort Jackson Eight case became national news in 1969. Shortly after the case's conclusion, the army issued the first federal guidelines on dissent during the Vietnam era. Commanders at army posts around the country received an official directive, referred to as "Guidance on Dissent," that specifically addressed antiwar activity among soldiers and how best to handle it. In categorizing the different manifestations of dissent found on and around army posts, the directive listed the two most significant threats as "possession and distribution of political materials" and "coffeehouses."[44] In keeping with its overall strategy of quiet containment, the directive acknowledged that soldiers were technically permitted to visit coffeehouses and other "off-post gathering places," as they were entitled to constitutional protections that included freedom of speech and association. "Severe disciplinary action in response to a relatively insignificant manifestation of dissent," the directive continued, "can have a counter productive effect on other members of the Command, because the reaction appears out of proportion to the threat which the dissent represents. Thus, such disproportionate actions may stimulate further breaches of discipline."[45] Nonetheless, the directive also left a clear opening for local commanders to declare coffeehouses "off-limits" if they decided that "the activities taking place there include counseling members to refuse to perform duty or to desert, or otherwise involve acts with a significant adverse effect on soldier health, morale, welfare."[46]

After the Fort Jackson Eight were released from the stockade, the UFO coffeehouse experienced a conspicuous increase in harassment by undercover FBI agents, local police, and civilians. UFO staff members noticed "straight people trying to act real cool" and were well aware that, in the UFO, they were often surrounded by undercover police and government plants.[47] Often agents would show up at the UFO dressed in rather obvious "radical" garb, attempting to infiltrate the staff by volunteering for work and mouthing extreme leftist rhetoric. As one staff member later recalled, "They [undercover infiltrators] were so eager to be useful and accepted that whenever we had a really nasty chore, we'd just give it to one of them. I used to think I was really popular. It was only later that I learned all those guys were being paid to be my friends."[48]

Government records reveal that the UFO staff were right to be paranoid: throughout the few years of its existence in Columbia, the UFO coffeehouse was aggressively investigated by all levels of state, local, and federal government. The FBI supplied local police with information on social activities engaged in by UFO staff, hoping to arrest them on drug charges.[49] Federal agents collected detailed profiles on the staff's political beliefs, sexual preferences, and travel plans and attacked the coffeehouse's finances, sending information to the IRS that taxes had not been paid on admission fees for live performances.[50] In addition to the undercover infiltrators on volunteer duty, several plainclothes agents (a mixture of local police, army intelligence, and FBI) visited the coffeehouse daily,[51] and a rotating group of military police officers stood guard outside the UFO's doors to observe and take note of the coffeehouse's patrons.[52] The UFO's constant, nearly-comic endurance of government surveillance and infiltration was even noted by visiting writer Norman Mailer, who began his August 1969 lecture at the coffeehouse by sardonically asking any undercover agents in the audience to stand and identify themselves.[53]

The intense law enforcement campaign took a heavy toll on the UFO and its staff. The close relationship between authorities at Fort Jackson and local police allowed for a nearly endless variety of legal harassment. Colonel Angelo Perri was acting chief of staff at Fort Jackson during the height of the army's concern with the UFO problem. He later explained, "[We] just called the police department, the chief, and he closed the coffeehouse. And the way they did it... the fire department went in, and said, 'Ah! Fire hazard here, fire hazard there, you know, gotta be closed.' Whether it was true or not, you know, you could go to court and sue them to reopen it."[54] In addition to being shut down for fire hazards and other violations, the coffeehouse's staff members were often personally cited on similarly minor charges that nonetheless carried costly fines.

Robert Duane Ferré, a former air force officer and native of Rochester, New York, was manager of the UFO coffeehouse during this period of intense scrutiny and harassment in the latter half of 1969. Ferré had served a year in prison for refusing to go to Vietnam and joined the antiwar movement after his release, arriving in Columbia, South Carolina, after the Fort Jackson Eight case. In addition to his work at the UFO, he involved himself in antiwar activities at locations throughout Columbia, hoping to reach those soldiers from Fort Jackson who might not visit the coffeehouse. On August 1, 1969, Ferré and another UFO staff member, Chris Hannafan, went to Jimmy's Drive-In, a local movie spot popular among GIs, to hand out antiwar leaflets. During their visit they spoke with two AWOL soldiers who wanted advice on applying for conscientious objector status. The manager of the drive-in called military police, who arrested the two soldiers. Ferré and Hannafan were themselves charged with disorderly conduct, each fined $100, and sentenced to thirty days in the Columbia jail.[55]

As it gained attention, the UFO became the subject of significant local hostility, targeted by some of Columbia's most influential groups and individuals. In addition to the Elite Epicurean Restaurant's animosity toward the UFO's existence, many other local merchants regularly complained to police about the coffeehouse's loud music, sidewalks blocked by hippies, and "obscene" posters facing the street. One of the latter featured "grinning American soldiers admiring severed human heads and was captioned, in part, 'the Army can really fuck over your mind if you let it.'"[56] In late 1969 these merchants began circulating a petition stating that the UFO coffeehouse was a public nuisance whose hostile atmosphere intimidated their customers and damaged long-standing businesses.[57]

The owner of the Elite Epicurean Restaurant was reluctant to sign the petition, fearing that she would have to testify in court. She was nevertheless subjected to pressure from several different merchants as well as the minister of a nearby church, all of whom urged her to help close the UFO. The chief of police and several police captains, who regularly had their morning coffee at the Elite, also persistently advised her that the coffeehouse was a potentially dangerous nuisance and that shutting it down would be in the city's (not to mention the Elite's) best interest. In January 1970, she relented and signed the petition.[58]

Unlike the many antiwar and civil rights petitions that had been circulated in Columbia and at Fort Jackson over the preceding years, the petition to close the UFO coffeehouse had the support of the city's prominent businesses, church leaders, military authorities, and city hall and thus carried considerably more weight despite its comparatively scant twelve signatures. Shortly after gaining the Elite Epicurean Restaurant's signature of support, a grand jury issued an indictment and Judge Harry T. Agnew wrote an injunction calling for the UFO coffeehouse to be forcibly shut down. On January 13, 1970, Columbia police put a chain and padlocks across the UFO's front doors and arrested Duane Ferré; his wife, Merle Ferré (then eight months' pregnant); and fellow UFO staff members Leonard Cohen and William Balk. The indictment accused the coffeehouse of being "a disorderly, ill-governed place, where fighting, cursing, and loud noises generate a public nuisance, marijuana and other drugs have been bought, sold, or used on the premises, obscene material has been displayed, and minors have been corrupted."[59]

The UFO's closing, and its staff's ensuing trial, caused a considerable furor in Columbia. The defendants received support from the city's increasingly vocal antiwar and counterculture community. The Reverend Gonzalo Leon, a local eccentric known for his bare feet, flowing hair, and stewardship of a New Age spiritual center called the Universal Life Church, became one of the coffeehouse's biggest champions, leading a series of rallies throughout the spring of 1970 in defiance of the city's attempt to shut it down. Other supporters raised constitutional arguments against the UFO's forced closure. Jon Kraus, an instructor at the University of South Carolina's Department of International Studies and president of the state's chapter of the American Civil Liberties Union, led a rally on January 18, 1970, five days after the UFO's closure, expressing his outrage at what he called a "a blatant attempt at political repression."[60] Howard Levy, recently released after serving thirty-two months in federal prison for his defiance at Fort Jackson three years earlier, also spoke at the same rally, which began on the university campus before sending more than 300 people marching downtown. The demonstration culminated in front of the locked doors of the UFO coffeehouse in "one of the loudest, if not the largest, protest marches ever held in the city."[61]

The bizarre trial of the three UFO staff members (Merle Ferré was not charged due to her pregnancy) showcased Columbia's official disgust with the coffeehouse and the people who frequented it. That revulsion was represented by the city's lead prosecutor, Fifth Circuit solicitor John Foard, a physical embodiment of Columbia's connections to state, federal, and military leadership. Foard, a decorated World War II veteran, had been a prominent city prosecutor for eighteen years, gaining a reputation as something of a showman. By the late 1960s, he was one of the city's most visible and colorful public characters. His arguments at trial often turned into fiery sermons, with Foard singing hymns and dropping to his knees to beg juries for guilty verdicts.[62] In 1970 he aimed his biblical righteousness at the UFO coffeehouse, casting it as a demonic entity polluting a decent town. In Foard's opening remarks to the jury, he read aloud several passages from the *Berkeley Barb*, an underground newspaper found among many others at the UFO. He highlighted profane language and comic images featuring drugs and nudity. Any place that would distribute such material, he argued, must be a "cesspool of evil."[63]

Throughout the trial, Foard painted the coffeehouse and its staff as dangerous agitators from outside Columbia, bent on destroying the city's way of life. He accused the UFO of being "detrimental to the peace, happiness, lives, safety and good morals of the people of the State of South Carolina" by promoting drug use, loud music, and antiestablishment values.[64] Foard even sang a few verses from "The Old Rugged Cross" in his closing argument. Several editorials in the city's leading newspaper, the *State*, commended Foard's passion and expressed disgust with the UFO's patrons and staff. One citizen called them "immature rabble . . . self-proclaimed redeemers of social and political ills who mock democracy and its freedoms and who chant slogans dedicated to our destruction" and stated that such persons forfeit their constitutional liberties.[65] But the coffeehouse was not without its supporters; the *State* also printed many letters that defended the UFO and assailed the police department and Foard himself for unfairly singling out the coffeehouse when several bars and restaurants around town were known for loud, drunken fights and easily obtainable marijuana. Why would soldiers be barred from a coffeehouse while still permitted to visit bars and brothels? The trial, these supporters suggested, was clearly politically motivated.[66]

On April 27, 1970, the three defendants were convicted of operating a public nuisance, a misdemeanor offense that typically carried a sentence of no more than ninety days.[67] In delivering his sentence, however, Judge Harry T. Agnew used the opportunity to set an example for the state of South Carolina, fining the UFO coffeehouse $10,000 (equivalent to nearly $60,000 today) and ordering Duane Ferré, Leonard Cohen, and William Balk each to serve six years in prison. He defended the unusually harsh sentence in a statement that captured how deeply the UFO coffeehouse had offended Columbia's city leadership: "As I understand it, two of the defendants came from great distances to this community. I have wondered where we are headed in this country, and what the future holds for my own children. It concerns me. I certainly hope that they won't come under the influence of persons who will guide them in the direction that I feel individuals who frequented the UFO would guide them. A great number of young people from all over South Carolina were exposed to the teachings of the defendants and the people of South Carolina are not accustomed to teachings of people from New York and San Francisco, who rebel against our form of life."[68] Despite his apparent disgust with the UFO staff, Agnew released them pending appeal, and a year later the sentences were reduced in exchange for their acceptance of lifetime banishment from the state of South Carolina.[69] John Foard himself agreed to lighter treatment for the staff, later explaining that he had accomplished his main goal, the permanent closure of the UFO coffeehouse.[70]

THE UFO IN EXILE

The demise of the UFO coffeehouse initiated what would turn out to be Columbia's final explosion of antiwar demonstrations during the Vietnam era and showed how the coffeehouse had evolved into an important icon for many of Columbia's young people. Student activists at the University of South Carolina (USC), outraged at what they interpreted as a political assault, formed a group called the "UFO in Exile," meeting weekly in a student union building on campus called Russell House and organizing student support for the coffeehouse and its staff while the trial progressed. After Judge Agnew delivered the six-year sentences in April, Solicitor Foard publicly announced his intent to extend his campaign to the university campus, declaring an unofficial war on drugs, dissidents, and the UFO in Exile. He used his connections on the university board of trustees to instigate a series of campus drug raids, investigate the student newspaper for obscenity, and restrict access to the Russell House political meeting center while dozens of city police officers patrolled the campus, performing random searches and asking students for identification.[71]

Foard's campaign, fueled by his seemingly personal grudge against the UFO coffeehouse and its sympathizers, had a chilling effect on academic freedom in Columbia.[72] Several college professors had testified in court on the UFO's behalf, and Foard sent letters to their respective departments, claiming that because of their testimony they "don't belong at the university."[73] Administrations at the city's various colleges actually followed through on some of Foard's recommendations. History professor Seldon Smith was subjected to an extensive fitness hearing at which his involvement with the UFO figured prominently; Smith had tenure and was ultimately retained by Columbia College. Other professors, however, did not fare so well. Ray Moore, a Methodist minister and untenured English instructor at Columbia College, was terminated based on the UFO trial transcript provided by Foard, as was prominent UFO supporter and untenured USC professor Jon Kraus. Several other instructors and professors reported being interrogated in the wake of the coffeehouse trial.[74]

Foard's heavy-handed effort to "clean up" the university in the wake of the coffeehouse trial coincided with the weeks of outrage on college campuses across the country over President Nixon's invasion of Cambodia and the subsequent killing of four students at Kent State on May 4. The confluence of national and local pressures was explosive in Columbia. Students at USC clashed with police and the National Guard throughout the first weeks of May 1970, with the demonstrations focused particularly on the city's repressive policies toward the UFO coffeehouse and its supporters at the college.[75] Russell House was the center of the storm on campus, as the building became, much like the UFO coffeehouse itself, a physical symbol for the students' struggle against authority. A series of escalating confrontations at Russell House eventually devolved into violence, with hundreds of students tear-gassed and beaten by National Guardsmen on May 11 and 12.

While antiwar rallies at USC had historically drawn very small crowds on campus, the demonstrations in 1970 against Foard and the police brought thousands of students to Columbia's streets. Even traditionally conservative campus institutions like fraternities and sororities joined in protests against police harassment after Governor Robert McNair asserted that "dorms are not sanctuaries" and authorized police to enter student housing buildings to search for drugs.[76] Just as in the Fort Jackson Eight case, the majority of student demonstrators and their sympathizers were not dedicated radicals. Many had never been to a demonstration before. They saw the attack on the UFO coffeehouse and the police occupation of the university as parts of a disturbing trend in Columbia that directly threatened its citizens' constitutional liberties.

As a local historian notes, "The antiwar movement in Columbia peaked and collapsed during the first part of 1970."[77] The UFO coffeehouse was a significant factor in that peak and collapse. During its two years of existence in Columbia, it was known, for better or worse, as the center of the city's developing counterculture and antiwar movements. The coffeehouse's evolution through several different distinct phases reflects the chaotic landscape of political and cultural possibilities that defined the era. The severe repression it faced, and the specific shape that repression took in Columbia, demonstrates how city, state, and federal authorities saw the coffeehouse's presence as extremely threatening. Its final collapse in a public trial helped trigger the largest student insurrection in the city's history.

When Fred Gardner opened the UFO in January 1968, just two years earlier, he certainly anticipated that an explicitly antiwar, counterculture coffeehouse would cause a stir in Columbia. That was, of course, part of its intended purpose. Arriving in town around the same time that the Orangeburg massacre brought national media attention to South Carolina's racial conditions, the coffeehouse quickly became popular among civil rights activists, dissident college students, and antiwar soldiers from Fort Jackson, who immediately employed the space as a safe house for political discussion and organization.[78] The chapel pray-in action, the formation of GIs United Against the War in Vietnam, and the defense of the Fort Jackson Eight case were all centrally planned at, and supported by, the UFO coffeehouse.

The UFO's closing, the prosecution of its staff, and the ensuing police crackdown at USC were all coordinated by the state police, military authorities at Fort Jackson, and the FBI.[79] Solicitor John Foard's public crusade against drugs and youthful radicalism helped him win reelection in the fall of 1970 in a campaign that promoted his closing of the UFO as one of the landmark events in his tenure.[80] Although Foard adamantly denied that his prosecution of the UFO was politically motivated and that he had never cooperated with federal authorities, government records detail Foard's close relationship with army authorities at Fort Jackson as well as substantial contact between Foard's office and the Committee on Internal Security, which at the time was charged with investigating subversion within the armed forces.[81] The coffeehouse's closure clearly served different purposes for different groups; nevertheless, the structures of power in Columbia, South Carolina, including the U.S. military at Fort Jackson, worked together to achieve the common goal of shutting down the UFO. For GI and civilian activists, the coffeehouse's forced closing was demoralizing but unsurprising, part of the wave of harassment and repression that every GI coffeehouse project, to varying degrees, experienced throughout the network's brief existence.

Moving On

A Changing War, a Changing Army, and a Changing Movement

> Despite the army's attempts to crush the GI movement, dissent within the ranks is growing, and will continue to grow as Nixon escalates the war in Southeast Asia and intensifies his crackdown here at home. But though expanding rapidly, the GI movement can't reach its full potential without active civilian support.
>
> *Fatigue Press* pamphlet (June 1970)

NIXON'S WAR

Richard Nixon's 1968 presidential campaign hinged to a large degree on his promise to de-escalate the nation's military involvement in Vietnam. Pledging to bring "an honorable end to the war," Nixon was responding to its deep unpopularity with the American public while simultaneously appealing to the revulsion toward antiwar protests, racial unrest, and counterculture felt by the Americans who made up his "silent majority."[1] After winning the presidency, Nixon and his administration pursued policies that significantly altered both the course of the war and the structure of the American military itself. As GI and civilian activists navigated a rapidly shifting political landscape, the force and direction of military antiwar activism underwent a considerable evolution.

Nixon's "Vietnamization" policy substantially rearranged America's war strategy. To withdraw ground troops, Nixon focused on the air war, placing much more of the burden of fighting on the navy and air force. As this bombing strategy unfolded, political resistance among active-duty soldiers shifted from the army to these other branches. Underground newspapers began appearing in unprecedented numbers at air force and navy bases around the country in 1970, reflecting the specific concerns of servicemen and servicewomen in these newly mobilized branches. The air force especially saw a dramatic rise in the kinds of phenomena that, in the war's earlier stages, had been concentrated in the army. In 1971, air force desertion rates doubled, and that summer serious incidents of organized insubordination disrupted the operations of five different air force bases.[2]

In addition to shifting the war's direction, Nixon's administration also took action to abolish the country's draft system entirely, pledging to convert the military to an all-volunteer system of recruitment at the conclusion of the Vietnam War.[3] A diverse public debate had intensified during the 1960s, as the war's operation raised serious questions about the fairness and efficacy of the draft system.[4] The Vietnam-era draft resistance movement, which developed through the 1960s and early 1970s, played a large part in publicizing the system's racial and economic imbalances, as the sight of young men burning their draft cards, taking refuge in churches, and risking arrest and imprisonment to protest the draft system helped bring the issue to the front of national political debate.[5] Over the course of the war, a number of military officials also began to support the idea of converting to an all-volunteer system. The Vietnam War's unpopularity had created practical problems for the armed forces, as reenlistment numbers began to drop precipitously after 1965.[6] With fewer young draftees choosing to stay in the army beyond the minimum requirement, some military leaders worried that the draft was creating an organization with a revolving door of unhappy, unmotivated soldiers, undermining the military's long-term strength and stability. In the 1968 presidential election, both major candidates supported the end of the draft system.

To facilitate the transition to an all-volunteer system, in January 1971 the army initiated a program known as VOLAR (Volunteer Army). The program was, in part, an attempt to address some of the common, everyday dissatisfactions with army life. At four different U.S. Army posts, the VOLAR program introduced a series of "adjustments to administrative and training practices, regulations, and policies governing individual lifestyle and working conditions," which were meant to make the army "a more satisfactory place in which to work by fostering professionalism, identification with the Army, and greater job satisfaction." Army leadership hoped that a more relaxed environment would not only attract more new recruits but also induce more soldiers who were already in the army to make a career out of it.[7]

As part of the VOLAR program, the army began opening its own GI coffeehouses on bases around the country. At Fort Hood, for example, where the Oleo Strut coffeehouse in Killeen had become a popular hangout for local GIs, officials used VOLAR funds to open an on-post coffeehouse called the Right Side in October 1971. The army's coffeehouse, whose name derived from a passage in the New Testament, was promoted as a place for soldiers to "relax . . . meet friends . . . or just to have a quiet place to think or pray." At a ribbon-cutting ceremony that opened the coffeehouse, Fort Hood major general James C. Smith explained that its purpose was to "involve the men of the division in the concerns about what is going on around them."[8] At Fort Carson, the Home Front coffeehouse in nearby Colorado Springs had, by 1971, become one of the most popular antiwar GI coffeehouses in the country. When Jane Fonda visited the post with a group of antiwar activists in 1971, local GIs gave them a grand tour of the new VOLAR-improved facilities, including Fort Carson's own psychedelic—but not antiwar—GI coffeehouse, the Inscape. As Fonda later recalled, she and many of the Carson soldiers with whom she spoke agreed that the Inscape had been created "to keep the men from coming to the GI movement coffeehouse."[9] The Inscape's walls were adorned with posters of pinup girls and advertisements for "girlie shows" featuring Playboy playmates. On the pages of *Life* magazine, photos of the army's coffeehouse depict a large crowd of soldiers sipping drinks at small tables, most of them staring up at a pair of bikini-clad go-go dancers shaking their hips on stage. With the army unrolling flashy attempts to win the hearts and minds of its soldiers, GI and civilian organizers recognized the need to adapt their movement to the VOLAR program and the wider set of policy changes initiated by Nixon's administration.

The antiwar movement's composition and strategies also changed significantly during the Nixon years. While popular memory often locates 1968 as the peak year of antiwar activism, in fact the post-1968 period witnessed some of the movement's most important developments. As sociologist and political historian Penny Lewis explains, "Post-1968 is the period when the movement formed deeper roots among people of color, religious communities, labor unions, the armed forces, veterans, and students attending second-, third-, and fourth-tier college campuses. The post-1968 rationales for opposing the war shifted from the more historically minded policy critiques and moral condemnations of the early years to include more explicitly grounded criticisms of the varied domestic repercussions of the fight."[10] GI coffeehouses and the wider GI movement were part of this evolution of ideas and tactics in the later years of the war. They took the GI movement in a number of new directions, as the influence of 1970s identity politics (particularly black liberation ideology and the women's movement) expanded the focus of antiwar activism. While these developments undoubtedly contributed to stronger divisions among activists in the coffeehouse network's later years, they also helped the coffeehouses become more dynamic political institutions.

The changing character of the GI movement and its civilian supporters could be seen at a series of movement-wide conferences held during the war's later years. According to reports from organizers, the movement's first two conferences, held in December 1969 and May 1970, were dominated by civilian radicals (mainly white males) who had "worked previously in the student and New Left movements," with very few active-duty GIs and veterans present. The conference held in November 1971 in Williams Bay, Wisconsin, however, almost totally reversed this imbalance; nearly fifty GIs and veterans attended the meetings, far outnumbering their civilian counterparts. The civilian wing had also undergone significant changes, with organizers reporting a "greater percentage of people from blue collar working class backgrounds" as opposed to the middle-class college students who had composed the majority of activists at previous meetings. They also reported an influx of women at various GI projects, whose presence helped contribute to an increased focus on gender issues both inside and outside the military.[11] From the perspective of GI and civilian organizers, these developments helped strengthen their movement, making it possible to address a wider set of issues related to military life than ever before.

During a time when most Americans understood the war in Vietnam to be finally winding down, GI and civilian activists were continuing, and even expanding, their operations. The war's ongoing impact on soldiers fueled a rising GI movement in the early 1970s. Alongside their antiwar activism, though, soldiers and civilians in this period addressed many other matters, including racial discrimination, drug abuse, housing practices, and the army's complicated conversion to an all-volunteer force. Coffeehouses were central to these new political directions, helping bring the GI movement to the peak of its influence during the war's final years.

"WHY DON'T YOU WRITE AN ARTICLE?": COFFEEHOUSES AND THE GI PRESS EXPLOSION

In June 1969, just a few months into Nixon's first term, the administration announced that 25,000 troops would return from Vietnam by the end of

August. To emphasize this point, the Department of Defense staged a "homecoming" ceremony in Tacoma, Washington, where Fort Lewis and its connected bases had been serving as the nation's main processing center for troops both going to and arriving from the Vietnam War. On July 8, 1969, when 814 American GIs arrived from Southeast Asia at nearby McChord Air Force Base, they were greeted by a group of dignitaries who included army chief of staff (and former commanding general of the war in Vietnam) William Westmoreland,[12] ambassador to South Vietnam Bui Diem, and Tacoma mayor A. L. Rasmussen. Adding a festive touch to the occasion was a brass band and a group of beauty queens and princesses from the Washington State area. The war-weary soldiers of the Third Battalion, Sixtieth Infantry, Ninth Infantry Division listened as Westmoreland gave a speech before they were bused to nearby Fort Lewis for the traditional postwar steak dinner. The group of GIs were then informed that in the morning they would begin training for their appearance in a larger "homecoming parade" to be held in downtown Seattle just two days later. The parade's utility as state propaganda was not lost on even mainstream media sources like the *New York Times*, which noted that, on the same day that the Third Battalion landed at McChord, 1,000 fresh troops were on the same tarmac boarding planes bound for the war zone, and an additional 10,000 soldiers would follow them in the month of July alone.[13]

The local and national media were not the only ones to call attention to the incongruity of the Nixon administration's Seattle parade. A significant number of antiwar activists were present at the event, many of whom held signs bearing slogans like "Welcome Home! We'll Stay in the Streets Until ALL of the GIs are Home!" and "Bring All the GIs Home Now!" A group of young women handed flowers to passing soldiers, many of whom accepted the tokens and flashed peace signs in return. Later in the evening, when the troops left the Seattle Center after a dinner of salmon and beer, antiwar activists waiting outside distributed leaflets and GI underground newspapers that urged soldiers to consider how the parade had employed them as political pawns.[14]

Challenging the administration's official narrative, the GI underground press became enormously influential over the course of the war. Beginning in 1967, a handful of GI-produced antiwar newspapers appeared on bases and in military towns. By 1972, the Department of Defense estimated that 245 different antiwar newspapers were being distributed on bases. Some of the most well-known GI papers, such as the *Fatigue Press* out of Killeen, Texas, and *Bragg Briefs* out of Fayetteville, North Carolina, which each had circulations of more than 5,000, were produced and distributed at GI coffeehouses, supported by civilian antiwar organizations.[15] Coffeehouses served as the meeting spaces and publishing centers for a loose national network of antiwar, military-oriented newspapers that formed, in the words of one historian and GI movement activist, "the fundamental expression of political opposition within the armed forces" during the Vietnam War era.[16]

The GI underground press was part of the larger history of newspaper printing, which underwent significant changes in the mid-twentieth century, deeply affecting the trajectory of New Left and antiwar groups in the Vietnam era. The introduction of new technologies, like cheap offset printing and mimeograph machines, helped make possible an unprecedented expansion of alternative media. Underground publications like the *Los Angeles Free Press*, the *Berkeley Barb*, and the *Chicago Seed* became significant agents in the promotion of a youth-oriented, antiwar counterculture that ran parallel to the so-called mainstream media. For most editors and producers of underground newspapers, the papers' physical production was itself a political act; to possess a printing press in the 1960s was to possess a new and powerful weapon in the movement's arsenal. The spaces where underground newspapers were produced, in which independent editors and writers gathered to discuss articles, exchange information, and physically print the newspaper, often became local centers of political organizing activity. More often than not, underground newspaper offices functioned as simultaneous publishing houses and de facto movement centers.[17]

Access to physical space and printing technology was a critical element in the explosion of social movements of the 1960s and 1970s, but it was especially critical in the development of the GI movement and its underground press network. The Uniform Code of Military Justice, whose rules applied in all branches of the military, stated that GIs could express their opinions in print only if they did so "off post, on their own time, with their own money and equipment."[18] Further, soldiers were restricted from preparing or distributing literature that included criticism of superior officers or members of government, including the president, the vice president, and members of Congress. As the number of GI antiwar newspapers showing up on U.S. military bases increased dramatically in 1968, military leadership issued even stricter policies limiting soldiers' ability to produce antiwar literature. The Department of the Army's "Guidance on Dissent" contained a token affirmation of GIs' "rights to free expression" but further limited those rights by stipulating that all printed materials be submitted to local commanders for approval before distribution.[19] While enforcement of these policies varied from post to post, subject to the whim of local commanders, GI organizers had good reason to tread carefully when producing and distributing literature.

Paul Cox, an active-duty Marine stationed at Camp Lejeune, North Carolina, along with two other soldiers, started a small underground paper called *Rage* after returning from Vietnam in 1969. Cox recalled that, because of local military restrictions, the success of a GI press was dependent on several related factors: the availability of an off-post workspace, access to printing technology, and financial support from civilians:

> There were three of us. We started writing letters to everyone we could find, asking for help. Two hundred forty-three letters. We got two responses. One was from *Bragg Briefs* in Fayetteville and one was from *Up Against the Bulkhead* in San Francisco. We got a visit from the people in Fayetteville, who recruited two guys to move into town. They got some money from somewhere and bought a house—they figured no one would rent to us—and opened a bookstore to support our work putting out this paper. There was a movement that was intent on assisting with the awakening of GIs. The U.S. Servicemen's Fund—we would send them a completed paper and they would send us $100. The first one, we mimeographed five hundred. Then we found a printer and went to tabloid, printing a thousand.[20]

Rage was one of many GI newspapers that benefited greatly from the material support of antiwar civilians, who were often able to provide the essential tools needed to make up for the severe limitations placed on soldiers' political expression.

At the Oleo Strut coffeehouse, where the *Fatigue Press* offices took up nearly half the space, the staff worked to create an atmosphere that would stimulate work on the newspaper. Vietnam veteran and *Fatigue Press* editor Dave Cline later explained that the coffeehouse staff encouraged visiting GIs to express their opinions in writing, regardless of their training or skills. "We started writing the paper, and the idea was for people just to write their ideas. When you would go in the coffeehouse, they would say, 'Why don't you write an article?' It was mimeographed, and the production was piss poor, but the idea was that we were putting something out."[21] The *Fatigue Press* ultimately became one of the country's most widely circulated GI papers, largely because of strong financial support from the USSF and other antiwar organizations that considered the Oleo Strut's role as an underground publishing center to be one of its most important functions. Activists at these organizations were encouraged when *Fatigue Press*'s coverage of Operation Garden Plot, Fort Hood's training operation for quelling urban riots, helped stir outrage among GIs on post and led to some of the GI movement's most effective early political actions.

The GI underground press also developed a unique political aesthetic, using the visual iconography, crass humor, smart-aleck attitude, and psychedelic imagery of the 1960s counterculture to subvert, provoke, and educate its readers. Many papers self-consciously copied the look and attitude of popular counterculture publications like the *Berkeley Barb* and *East Village Other*, connecting the GI movement's politics to the subversive humor of 1960s youth culture. Having grown up reading *Mad* magazine and its many antecedents, artists in GI underground newspapers persistently used the comic medium to make fun of the military establishment. Virtually every GI paper contained over-the-top comic images satirizing military authority.[22]

The most common target of these comics were "lifers," the GI movement's preferred term for career military men. In contrast to enlisted GIs, officers were not simply serving their required time before discharge but had made a career out of military service. The large numbers of "lifers" during the Vietnam era was the result of the military's post–World War II policy shifts that promoted the army as a viable career. As the Cold War expanded in the early 1950s, the Officer Corps, which functioned as the army's central group of "middle managers," grew to become the centerpiece of a new and more professional military. It was during this period that the army began advertising the "military career" as a way to express patriotism while earning a living. By the Vietnam War era, the increased numbers of career officers meant greater competition for jobs and promotions, which helped contribute to an atmosphere of behavioral conformity, including a pressure to align their attitudes with the goals and ethos of the military establishment.[23]

As the Vietnam War brought an unprecedented number of draftees into the U.S. military, frequent clashes between enlisted GIs and officers became symptomatic of larger class, racial, and generational divides in the nation's armed forces. A GI stationed in Vietnam, when interviewed in the *New York Times*, expressed a seemingly common sentiment: "The grunt's the one who has to go through all the hell[;] . . . lifers sit back in their air-conditioned rooms" and tell GIs to "go out there and fight the war" while they "draw their combat pay for doing nothing while they're sitting on their butts."[24]

Since so much of this tension stemmed from the war's unpopularity, the enlisted soldier/officer divide took on particular resonance for antiwar GIs.

According to psychiatrist and writer Robert Jay Lifton, for soldiers opposed to the war and alienated by military values, career officers came to signify "not only the counterfeit universe of the immediate environment and the larger military establishment, but also the misguided older generation responsible for sending him to fight the war, and indeed for the war itself."[25] During the late 1960s and early 1970s, officers were depicted on the pages of GI underground newspapers as pigs, rabid dogs, grotesque old men, and, in at least one case, anthropomorphized toilets. By targeting "lifers," the GI movement expressed its contempt for the entire concept of military service, using cultural differences (crew cuts versus long hair, alcohol versus marijuana, country music versus rock and roll) to cast traditional military values (and those who willingly embraced them) as hopelessly old-fashioned, square, and out of touch with the younger generation. These images, along with countless articles, editorials, and letters printed in the GI underground press during the Vietnam era, were a powerful reflection of the military's "morale crisis," providing visual evidence of a cultural breakdown that alarmed military leaders and led to substantial policy changes. With coffeehouses serving as its central production and distribution centers, the GI press created a brief but remarkable phenomenon on military posts around the country, providing GIs with an unrelenting stream of alternative information and perspectives.

RACE AND IDENTITY POLITICS

The solidarity on display in underground GI newspapers could often obscure some of the bitter divisions within the GI movement, whose trajectory was shaped profoundly by the turbulent internal politics of the New Left in the later years of the Vietnam War. Much of this turbulence concerned the rising tide of Black Power, black nationalism, and Third World solidarity that challenged predominantly white left organizations to reshape their foundational ideologies and organizational strategies. The New Left had found its early inspiration in the civil rights movement of the late 1950s and early 1960s, as young whites had sought to join the cause of racial integration with their own liberal vision of "participatory democracy." But by 1966, after Stokely Carmichael coined the phrase "Black Power" at a Mississippi civil rights march led by the vanguard Student Nonviolent Coordinating Committee, white and black radicals increasingly viewed each other from across a racial divide. Less than a week after Carmichael's Black Power speech, Students for a Democratic Society president Todd Gitlin issued a statement affirming the leading student activist organization's support for Black Power, which essentially asserted that white radicals, rather than pursue integration, should seek to "organize their own communities" and address racism at its source.[26] Though generally sympathetic to surging black radicalism, many of these organizations found themselves increasingly paralyzed by fierce internal battles in the late 1960s, unable to agree on the precise nature of the revolution they hoped to effect.

The war in Vietnam and the movement against it were similarly influenced by the wider atmosphere of racial struggle. In 1967, Martin Luther King Jr. delivered an iconic antiwar speech, "Beyond Vietnam," in which he connected the miserable social and economic situation of blacks in America to the suffering of Vietnamese peasants at the hands of the U.S. military. While he stopped short of urging black soldiers to defect, King nevertheless made it clear that service in Vietnam was especially problematic for young black men. According to King, the war was taking men "who had been crippled by our society and sending them eight thousand miles away to guarantee liberties which they had not found in Southwest Georgia and East Harlem."[27] King's words pointed out a "cruel irony" that found potent expression among young black GIs in the Vietnam-era armed services.

Perhaps no other figure more publicly represented the black experience of Vietnam than heavyweight champion boxer and international celebrity Muhammad Ali, whose principled stand against service in the war inspired countless young black men to find their own paths of resistance. His notorious retort "I ain't got no quarrel with the Vietcong. No Vietcong ever called me Nigger" seemed to cut right to the heart of the matter and strengthened the notion that, for many black men, fighting in the war represented a serious betrayal of racial and class identity. Employing logic similar to King's and other black leaders', Ali pointed out, "Why should they ask me to put on a uniform and go ten thousand miles from home and drop bombs and bullets on brown people in Vietnam while so-called Negro people in Louisville are treated like dogs and denied simple human rights?"[28] As this attitude became more prominent among young black GIs, the military itself became one more front in the battle to confront institutionalized racism.[29]

The powerful influence of racial ideology was felt at GI coffeehouses around the nation, with several GI projects confronting the same set of complex racial issues that challenged many radical groups during the late 1960s and early 1970s. The Movement for a Democratic Military (MDM), for example, quickly rose to become one of the largest coffeehouse-initiated GI projects in the country, until it was unable to sustain itself in the face of significant racial division. The MDM was founded in 1970 in a popular GI coffeehouse called the Green Machine, located near Camp Pendleton, the major West Coast base of the U.S. Marine Corps, in San Diego, California. The group published an important and widely read GI newspaper, *Attitude Check*, which spelled out a basic list of revolutionary demands that became common political positions among GI movement activists around the country, even well after the MDM disintegrated. These demands included the recognition of constitutional rights for all soldiers, the right to collective bargaining, freedom for all political prisoners, an end to institutional racism, a complete overhaul of the Uniform Code of Military Justice, and, of course, an immediate and total withdrawal of American troops from Vietnam.[30] Six different military bases established MDM chapters in the early months of 1970, prompting Marine commandant general Leonard Chapman, in an interview with a military affairs magazine, to label the organization "a serious threat to the defense of this country."[31]

Contrary to Chapman's fears, a power struggle for control of the MDM in San Diego resulted in its total collapse after little more than a year of activity. The MDM's disintegration was entirely about race; black editors at *Attitude Check* split from the MDM to form their own GI paper, *Black Unity*. In its first issue, the editors delivered a concise statement of the difficulties that plagued the GI movement as factionalism of all sorts increasingly disrupted efforts to create a unified mass movement of soldiers: "The reason why MDM separated and *Attitude Check* won't be around anymore is because we weren't getting the full support of people. Third World people (black, brown, red, yellow) couldn't relate to it because they thought it was a white organization. White people couldn't relate to it because they thought it was a black struggle. We are all struggling to reach the same goals, but we each have to organize our own people first. Once we organize among ourselves, then we can unite. Until all of us are free, none will be free."[32] Like many radical organizations during this period, the members of MDM were united in their opposition to the Vietnam War and shared many of the same political objectives but were unable to overcome the bitter racial barriers that divided their movement.

The Oleo Strut coffeehouse similarly experienced significant racial difficulties in the later years of its existence. Strut staff members were initially elated at the formation of the Fort Hood United Front, an organization of black and white GIs working together on antiwar activities on post and in the surrounding community. However, because of the potent racial hostilities at

Fort Hood, and in the spirit of self-determination then permeating the black movement, a group of black soldiers decided that it was necessary to create an all-black GI organization. When in the fall of 1971 this group split off from the United Front to form the People's Justice Committee, racial tensions at the coffeehouse came bubbling to the surface. The new committee held a few meetings at the Oleo Strut, initially expressing hope of working together with Strut activists, but after several black GIs objected to the Strut for being, among other things, "dominated by whites," the group stopped frequenting the coffeehouse and began meeting instead at a local USO (United Service Organizations) office.[33] Since so much of the antiwar and radical energy at Fort Hood was located within its population of young black soldiers, most of whose political sensibilities were deeply informed by Black Power and similar ideologies, the Oleo Strut's reputation as a meeting place for primarily white activists directly affected its ability to build solidarity with one of the most active wings of the local GI movement.

At the November 1971 GI movement conference in Williams Bay, Wisconsin, organizers attempted to chart a course through the political and racial divisions then hindering the development of many GI projects. At a moment when black GIs were becoming the driving force of GI activism, the stereotypical image of coffeehouses as hangouts for white middle-class peace activists presented a distinct challenge for GI organizers. At a workshop on racism and Third World struggles, representatives from several different coffeehouses reported significant racial problems, echoing the experiences of the Oleo Strut and Green Machine projects. There was consensus among the participants that civilian-sponsored GI projects, in military towns around the country, had difficulties sustaining relationships with "non-white" soldiers, despite black soldiers' particularly strong antiwar and radical sentiments: "It seemed clear that while there had been working alliances between the projects and the black groups at their bases, ... there had been no continuous ongoing black participation in the projects."[34]

The activists at the conference were well aware of racial problems at GI coffeehouses but were unsure about how to address them. One glaring issue was the composition of the conference itself; a published summary later admitted that "similar to early conferences ... the organizers were, again, overwhelmingly white." At the workshop devoted specifically to racial issues, only one black activist was present in a room that contained more than two dozen white organizers. According to the meeting minutes, the lone black activist "spoke for a long time about the different things that make it difficult for blacks and other minorities to relate to white organizers and organizations. Among these were class and race problems. There was a strong feeling that our relations with black and third world brothers and sisters hadn't been satisfactory to us or them either on a personal or a political level."[35] Though the racism workshop ended with a series of vague resolutions ("Never tolerate racism" among them) and promises to encourage racial unity, organizers recognized that the coffeehouse network had been unable to escape the infighting and racial division that were fracturing the antiwar movement and the New Left in the later stages of the Vietnam War.

DRUGS AND COUNTERCULTURE

GI and civilian activists at GI coffeehouses also frequently clashed over the issue of drugs, reflecting a common thread among radicals of the era. On the one hand, drug culture had been, for many activists, an entry into an alternative mode of thought and behavior that had led them directly to political activism. Marijuana and LSD, prominent in the youth counterculture of the 1960s, were viewed by many young people as useful tools of revolution, liberating minds on the way to developing a new, more humane American society. But the drug counterculture's vision of how to make social change created significant conflict within the antiwar movement, particularly in New Left organizations like Students for a Democratic Society, whose leaders fretted that the counterculture's narcotic escapism would siphon energy from important political activities.[36]

Coffeehouse organizers were also well aware that their activities were under constant surveillance by law enforcement and other unknown entities and took steps to eliminate the possibility of arrest by running as "clean" an operation as possible. This meant keeping drugs away from the coffeehouses at all costs. USSF newsletters consistently underlined the importance of a strict "no drugs" policy at all coffeehouse projects. It is impossible to know exactly how much these policies were adhered to, but it is clear that most GI coffeehouses went out of their way to warn their staff and patrons, both verbally and in print, that the coffeehouses were deceptively "safe" environments, where possession of drugs ("holding") came with a significantly elevated risk of getting arrested.

Before a rock concert at the Oleo Strut in Killeen, Texas, in 1968, for example, coffeehouse manager Josh Gould announced the rules to a packed house, making reference to the assumed presence of undercover agents: "Rule one:

We got no holding in the place. If you're holding, it's a bad place to be. The sign over there says that the Man is welcome, and always remember, the Man *is* welcome here. But it's not so much that he's welcome, it's just that he's *here*."[37] In newspaper articles announcing the opening of the Fort Knox Coffeehouse in Muldraugh, Kentucky, the organizers similarly discouraged drugs based on the obvious dangers of arrest: "There is only one rule at the Coffee House: No drugs, liquor or fights. The brass would like nothing better than to close us down, declare the place off-limits, or attempt to harass people. These would give them and the local police the opportunity to do so, let's not give them that chance."[38] And in candid terms, the activists at the Covered Wagon in Mountain Home, Idaho, articulated the coffeehouse's drug policy by explaining how it related to their larger mission: "There is one firm rule at the Wagon. NO DOPE IS ALLOWED. If you want to get ripped before coming that is your business and your responsibility. But we don't intend to violate any small laws. A dope bust interferes with our effort to change the entire system and build instead something that is responsive to human needs."[39]

Drugs were a regular topic of discussion among organizers at GI coffeehouses. At the time, heroin addiction was a major problem within the army, another distressing symptom of the toll the Vietnam War was taking on GI morale. While radicals may have quibbled about the positive potential of drugs like marijuana and LSD, there was little disagreement about the toxic physical and psychological effects of heroin and opiate addiction, and coffeehouse organizers struggled (as would the military itself) to address this complicated crisis. At the Haymarket Square Coffeehouse in Fayetteville, North Carolina, outside Fort Bragg, the staff reported in 1971 that "drugs have been a constant hassle" since the coffeehouse became the favorite hangout of a large group of "street people" who were young, homeless, and often addicted to harder drugs like heroin ("skag"). Their presence created serious conflict among the Haymarket's civilian organizers. Since they were the only group of people in Fayetteville who seemed to identify and sympathize with the coffeehouse's outsider status and political mission, some staff members were hesitant to alienate them, feeling that their natural antiauthoritarianism could be channeled into serious political action. Others at the coffeehouse disagreed, arguing that the young people hanging out at the Haymarket were hard, manipulative, insincere, isolated individuals who drained resources from the coffeehouse's mission of organizing GIs.[40]

While the activists at the Haymarket Square Coffeehouse could never agree on how to employ the local drug culture within their wider political strategy, their ambivalence points to a common problem within the GI coffeehouse movement: how to capitalize on the popularity of a drug-inspired counterculture, using it to attract antiwar-leaning GIs, while simultaneously discouraging actual drug use. It was a difficult balance to strike, leading to many admittedly comical disagreements, like the one involving the "Spinning Light Committee," which formed at the Oleo Strut coffeehouse to agitate for the return of a psychedelic display that had been removed by the staff in an effort to discourage drug-induced hypnotic escapism.[41] The Strut staff, like the organizers at the Haymarket, recognized the "dual nature" of drug culture and similarly failed to find a clear solution. As David Zeiger later explained, "You could say that a majority of GIs [at Fort Hood] 'relate' to dope and the culture, or pseudo-culture, that goes with it. What you could also say, though, is that the reason there is so much dope on Hood is because it is also one of the most oppressive bases in the country, and that dope serves to pacify GIs and prevent them from fighting back. The argument between these two theories has come up time and time again at the Strut, and the rule against dope has been consistently broken."[42]

The struggle over the drug issue brought up a larger question for coffeehouse organizers: did the coffeehouse's employment of a counterculture aesthetic and lifestyle actually help further their political goals? On this issue, many organizers discovered stark contradictions in their overall approach to GI organizing, finding that an overly enthusiastic embrace of the counterculture's "lifestyle as politics" could stand in the way of effective political work with soldiers. At the Oleo Strut, for example, the civilian staff, usually a group of ten or more, resided communally in a rented house in Killeen and self-consciously attempted to live out their politics of personal liberation, with mixed results. David Zeiger, reporting to the USSF, observed some of the basic conflicts this lifestyle created: "The staff did not work, day to day, with the people it was organizing—it was set apart from them, living some kind of completely different life, which gave the appearance to a lot of people of a hippie commune—no set hours, no need to face the Man every day, a real easy type life. It's impossible to live such a unique life from the people you are trying to build a movement with and still work with them on a close basis. . . . A question that has never been reconciled at the Strut is the conflict between 'personal' life and 'political' life."[43] Communal living arrangements, which were often formed as much out of financial necessity as political orientation, nevertheless seemed to cause problems at several coffeehouses, directly affecting the relationship between civilians and GIs. Organizers at the Haymarket Square Coffeehouse reported in 1971 that "collective living does tend to put us off from working people, by being such an oddity."[44]

By 1972, national GI coffeehouse support organizations like the USSF reached a consensus on the issue of "staff collectives." Based on the negative experiences of several coffeehouses around the nation, civilian activists concluded that their attempts to live out their politics in counterculture communes were actually hindering their larger mission of organizing antiwar soldiers:

> There was general agreement that the living collective is not a good form for several reasons: in most base towns it is so foreign to the local community that local residents tend to freak and respond negatively; GIs seem put off by it, because it is mostly different from their own experience; it creates a cliquish kind of exclusivity; and the appearance of sexual freedom offers a contradiction between the daily life of staff vs. that of GIs which is counterproductive.... Although strong economic motives exist for establishing a living collective, there are strong drawbacks for such an arrangement, including the inability of working people to relate to collectives ... and the tendency for such groups to be isolated from others in the project, especially GIs.[45]

After some experimentation, coffeehouse organizers realized that integrating the youth counterculture into their political project was a complicated undertaking; rather than promote solidarity among civilians and soldiers, the lifestyle of sex, drugs, and rock and roll could often serve inadvertently to highlight the differences between them.

"WE KNOW WHAT YOU'RE UP AGAINST AND WE SUPPORT YOU": THE FTA SHOW TOUR

Despite major disagreements about its appropriate role in the GI movement, organizers at GI coffeehouses recognized that youth counterculture was an important element in their overall strategy. Coffeehouse network founder Fred Gardner had always insisted that the coffeehouses were, above all, cultural institutions, offering soldiers a hip refuge from the stifling atmosphere found in the pool halls and dive bars that dominated most military towns.

Michael Uhl, a Fort Hood GI who became an antiwar activist after returning from Vietnam, discovered that the Oleo Strut coffeehouse was, for many soldiers in Killeen, the only game in town:

> I might not have started going there at all had the town offered any reasonable alternative. But after a few deadly evenings shooting pool, I cruised slowly past the Strut, and the scene there appeared leagues more inviting than anything Killeen's other leisure dives had to offer. The organizers had created an informal—but hip—cafe setting, where a spinning light on the ceiling strobed wall posters of rebel political icons.... Of the patrons, overwhelmingly off-duty GIs, a few had their noses buried in newspapers or magazines. The majority percolated around the small tables in animated conversation, while the activists who staffed the place, both male and female, circulated among them. Here was the antithesis of the non-verbal posturing and compulsive boozing that so typified the holding pens where most American servicemen spend their idle hours.[46]

To Fred Gardner, stories like Uhl's helped confirm that the counterculture was a significant part of the coffeehouse network's overall appeal.

Like Gardner, army veteran and antiwar activist Howard Levy was convinced that youth culture could be a revolutionary force in the American military. To this end, in the fall of 1971 Levy began formulating an idea for an antiwar-themed stage show for soldiers. He envisioned a kind of counterculture comedy revue that would reflect the political and cultural values of young soldiers who were turned off by the military's official entertainment. Most of all, thought Levy, the show would be a visible demonstration of the civilian antiwar movement's support for dissident soldiers.

For several decades, Bob Hope's USO show was the most popular, and most officially sanctioned, of the different kinds of entertainment offered to GIs at military bases around the world. The USO was chartered in 1941 in coordination with the Department of Defense, with a mission to provide "morale, recreation, and entertainment" services to American troops serving overseas.[47] Though not officially a part of the government, USO shows and related recreational events bring celebrities and other public figures into a war zone as a means of elevating morale. For a period of nearly fifty years, Bob Hope was the USO's chief entertainer, a ubiquitous presence on the scene of virtually every American military campaign of the era. Hope, a vaudeville comedian who became a Hollywood film star in the 1940s, first signed on to the USO show during World War II and, over the course of fifty years, evolved into the USO's most tireless performer (and, ultimately, a symbol of the USO itself). As *Time* magazine put it in 1967, "Bob Hope wasn't born—he was woven by Betsy Ross." On tour, Hope's performances blended comedy routines with musical acts and the obligatory scantily clad appearances by Miss USA and other pinup girls. With his signature golf club, faux bachelor persona, and obvious affection for military men and women, Hope served as the popular, smiling face of the American home front, sent to bring good cheer to soldiers and support staff in the heat of battle.[48]

By the late 1960s, though, many of Hope's old-fashioned jokes began to fall flat for audiences of young GIs, who often found Hope's show corny at best, offensive at worst. For the portion of those soldiers who were opposed to the war, the government-sponsored USO show seemed like a form of cultural propaganda that reinforced many of the values that had created the Vietnam War in the first place. In an attempt to win over the increasingly unreceptive crowds (particularly in Vietnam itself), in 1970 Hope introduced jokes about marijuana into his act and even claimed that he himself was antiwar (joking that he was "a hawk who's now turned chicken").[49] There were signs that many GIs saw through Hope's bid for cultural and political relevance, however. At one USO show performance in Saigon in 1970, a group of musically inclined soldiers employed their own countercultural form of expression, acid rock, to voice their disapproval. The GIs had been booked to play a set of songs before Hope came onstage. To the roar of the crowd, the soldiers announced, "We'd like to dedicate this to our childhood idol, Mr. Bob Hope," and immediately began playing their first song: Black Sabbath's searing heavy metal classic "War Pigs."[50]

In creating an antiwar alternative to Hope's USO performances, Levy hoped to create a show that would bring mainstream publicity to the GI movement. To that end, he wanted as much radical star power as the USSF could muster. At the time, Jane Fonda and Donald Sutherland were filming director Alan J. Pakula's *Klute* in New York City, where Levy maintained the USSF's main base of operations. Fonda had become deeply involved in supporting the GI movement since her tour of coffeehouses the previous year, and Levy was eager to enlist her support for his antiwar road show. Seeing an opportunity to combine her acting talents and Hollywood connections with her nascent radical politics, Fonda loved Levy's idea. The actors agreed to help the USSF sponsor a series of performances near military bases around the country, enlisting the support of their friends in Hollywood to create a separate organization, Entertainment Industry for Peace and Justice, which would assemble talent and coordinate resources for the show.[51] Writers and activists Jules Feiffer, Barbara Garson, and Herb Gardner (no relation to Fred) were charged with writing and developing a series of songs and skits to communicate an antiwar message with a countercultural sensibility. Co-opting the popular underground acronym found scrawled on the walls of military barracks around the world (though remaining coy about what the initials *really* stood for), the show would be called, simply, "FTA."[52] The FTA troupe planned to take their tour to major military bases around the United States, using GI coffeehouses as local bases of operation. Fred Gardner joined the FTA show as a stage manager and liaison to the coffeehouse staff.[53]

The FTA show's original planners envisioned a slyly subversive comedy show with broad appeal. The material had an undeniably serious antiwar subtext, but politics was always to take a back seat to entertainment. According to Levy, the goal was to create a series of performances that "could arguably be shown on base" as officially sponsored entertainment for troops, and FTA writers worked hard to fashion a "mainstream" show that avoided direct political provocation in favor of comedic barbs and light satire. By the spring of 1971, the troupe had developed a complete three-hour program and rehearsed in New York City for a few weeks before taking the show on the road.[54]

Before leaving New York in February, Fonda and Levy held a press conference announcing their intentions to kick off the FTA tour in Fayetteville, North Carolina, near Fort Bragg. They explained that Fort Bragg had been chosen as the first stop on the tour because its commanding officer, Lieutenant General John J. Tolson, played a significant role in the army's recently instituted experiments in "social liberalization," which allowed GIs to wear longer hair and mustaches in an attempt to ameliorate generational and cultural tensions within the military hierarchy.[55] The organizers saw the FTA show as the perfect opportunity to test the limits of Fort Bragg's newfound cultural permissiveness. Levy appealed directly to Tolson: "If General Tolson is really serious about the Army's so-called liberalization policy, and believes in the Army's 'new mod look,' he'll let our show on the base. If not, he will ban it, and let the public know it's the same old fashioned, repressive Army." Because Tolson was the "key architect of the Army's new look," Levy added with tongue partially in cheek, "we expect his full cooperation."[56]

After USSF organizers sent Tolson a script of the FTA show, he refused to allow it on base, describing the show's contents as "detrimental to discipline and morale." GIs at Fort Bragg reacted to the show's rejection by drawing up a petition to Congress, signed by more than 2,000 soldiers in a matter of days.[57] The ensuing publicity, largely the result of the involvement of antiwar celebrities, was an embarrassment for Tolson. When reporters asked him if he had banned Fonda and company from the base because of their antiwar politics, he replied that the FTA show was "not so much antiwar as poorly done."[58] Unsurprisingly, the show was subsequently banned from military bases across the nation; the search for usable performance space became a significant logistical hurdle for the show's national tour.

Since the whole point of the FTA show was to bring the maximum amount of publicity to the GI movement, its planners worked to make each show a major event for the military towns in which they intended to perform. Although GI coffeehouses seemed like the logical venues for FTA performances, with a ready-made staff of sympathetic civilians and GIs, organizers thought the coffeehouses were far too small to accommodate the kinds of massive crowds they hoped to attract and instead attempted to book the show in large public venues like high school auditoriums, civic centers, and performing arts halls. But the show's subversive reputation made many local leaders reluctant to allow their public institutions to host it. As the tour made its stops in cities across the country, GI coffeehouses often turned out to be the only spaces willing to accommodate Fonda and her traveling antiwar show.

In Fayetteville, for example, resistance to the FTA show was not limited to military leaders at Fort Bragg. When the show's planners submitted an application to use the city's 2,500-seat municipal auditorium, city officials initially rejected the proposal until a federal judge agreed with USSF lawyers and overruled the decision. The city then demanded $150,000 in insurance for the performance, a prohibitive expense for the USSF, and the first FTA show was finally held instead at the Haymarket Square Coffeehouse on March 14, 1971.[59] Since the coffeehouse only had room for fewer than five hundred people, the troupe put on a series of performances, to packed houses of GIs, over the course of two days and nights.

By most media accounts, the FTA show's premiere in Fayetteville was a huge hit among the soldiers who crowded into the coffeehouse. The performers included Fonda and fellow actors Donald Sutherland, Peter Boyle, and Elliot Gould, comedian Dick Gregory, folk singers Len Chandler and Barbara Dane, and rock acts Swamp Dogg and Johnny Rivers. The show itself embodied the antiestablishment, antiauthority attitude of the youth counterculture, with each song, comic routine, skit, or reading focusing on a different aspect of the Vietnam War and the GI experience. Gregory set the tone of the evening with his first joke, in which he suggested that GIs vote as a bloc to raise the draft age to seventy-five, to "send all them older cats to Vietnam with John Wayne leading 'em." Throughout the first performances at the Haymarket coffeehouse, hundreds of GIs clapped, sang along, and cheered loudly.[60]

Although the material was undeniably subversive, in general the FTA show favored light satire over radical political statements. Many of the jokes, about the unfairness of military hierarchy and the everyday annoyances of army life, would not be out of place in a *Beetle Bailey* comic strip or even in Bob Hope's ostensibly "pro-war" USO show. What made the FTA show different was that its performers were understood to be representatives of the civilian antiwar movement and the show itself was recognized as an explicitly political act. The performances demonstrated support for the varied forms of antiwar activism then being expressed by growing numbers of active-duty GIs on bases around the country. During the show's more serious moments, such as when Sutherland dramatically read from Dalton Trumbo's 1938 antiwar novel *Johnny Got His Gun*, the FTA troupe underlined the horrors of war, the specific injustice of Vietnam, and the responsibilities of citizen-soldiers to challenge the military power structure. But the show stopped short of proselytizing, instead expressing a kind of abstract solidarity with, and support for, soldiers who questioned the war. Fonda explained that the show reinforced "what the soldiers already know. *They know that the war is insane*. They know what GIs have to contend with better than we do. We're simply saying, 'We know what you're up against and we support you.'"[61]

While the FTA troupe saw their show as a relatively uncontroversial statement of support, military and local authorities often viewed Fonda's arrival as a significant threat to morale and security. On the weekend the show debuted in Fayetteville, Fort Bragg went into high alert, mobilizing fifty jeeps and trucks behind barracks and using military police to block access points to the base's stockade (where nearly half of the 173rd Airborne Brigade was confined).[62] The Haymarket Square Coffeehouse was inundated with plainclothes and undercover agents, many of them wearing "counterculture" disguises that were apparently easy to spot; Dick Gregory joked that GIs should be on the lookout for "spit-shine sandals." Groups of photographers, presumed to be police or federal agents, surrounded the coffeehouse throughout the performances, using infrared cameras to photograph soldiers in the crowd, coffeehouse staff, and, of course, Hollywood celebrities.[63] Fayetteville authorities were clearly alarmed by the FTA show's presence, unsure of its intentions, and hostile to its political message. The pattern of resistance displayed in Fayetteville, from its refusal to allow the use of its public facilities to the mobilization of its police force, was repeated in military towns throughout the FTA show's fall 1971 tour.

Organizers at the USSF, aware of the hostility the show faced in military towns, relied on local coffeehouse staff to survey the situation and help find friendly venues for performances. In Killeen, Texas, FTA show representatives alerted Oleo Strut staff members in July that the FTA show would be stopping by to entertain Fort Hood GIs in September and asked them to set to work looking for available spaces. Killeen's high school auditorium was one of the town's few venues capable of accommodating more than a thousand people. Although the coffeehouse staff had witnessed the auditorium hosting a number of religious and right-wing political events during their years in Killeen, the school board denied their request on the basis of the show's political content; a federal suit filed by USSF lawyers, similar to the one filed in Fayetteville, was unsuccessful. Killeen's movie theaters also refused to rent out their facilities. After the *Killeen Daily Herald* issued an editorial stating that Jane Fonda and her troupe should be legally barred from even stepping foot in town, the manager of the Oleo Strut reported that "looking for an alternative place to have the show . . . was like trying to find a Cuban cigar in Selma, Alabama."[64] When the show finally rolled into town, the Oleo Strut coffeehouse was literally the only place in Killeen that would welcome Fonda and the FTA group. They staged five smaller performances in the cramped coffeehouse for audiences of 200 to 300 GIs at each show. On Sunday, the troupe held a picnic in Killeen's Condor Park, where performers talked with soldiers and other activists for several hours before moving on to their next stop.[65]

More than 15,000 GIs saw the FTA show during its fall 1971 tour of U.S. military towns, despite often intense local efforts to disrupt it. The involvement of antiwar celebrities like Fonda and Sutherland created an unprecedented amount of publicity and media attention for the GI movement and helped reveal how widespread military discontent had become. By the time the FTA show arrived in Mountain Home, Idaho, in December 1971, a robust local antiwar movement was already underway among airmen and airwomen from Mountain Home Air Force Base. Together with USSF-sponsored civilian activists, they had finally managed to reopen their antiwar coffeehouse, the Covered Wagon, after the original was burned to the ground. The Covered

Wagon was unquestionably the center of antiwar activity in the tiny town of fewer than 10,000. The FTA show's packed performances at the coffeehouse suggested that antiwar sentiment was as powerful among air force personnel in 1971 as it had been in the army in 1968; wherever the burden of war shifted, desertion, insubordination, and antiwar activism among soldiers followed.[66] After the performance at the Covered Wagon, a reporter asked Fonda if her show encouraged air force servicemen to revolt. She responded, "No, they're ahead of us on that."[67]

While coffeehouses proved to be the only consistently reliable venues to hold performances throughout the FTA show's tour, local coffeehouse staff greeted the show's arrival with trepidation. Several coffeehouse organizers were skeptical of the show's intentions and overall value to the movement. David Zeiger, who managed the Oleo Strut coffeehouse during the FTA show's visit, later reported that GI projects were protective of the local movements they had been building and resented the FTA show's perceived arrogance: "The leadership of the show considered itself fully capable of passing judgment on projects that had been working and organizing for years; they also presented the picture of seeing the show as the most important thing going. The result was that there was some heavy conflict between the show and some of the projects."[68] Fred Gardner, in his role as liaison to the coffeehouses, often found himself in the middle of tensions between local activists and the FTA show's entourage of celebrities, press photographers, agents, lawyers, and support staff.[69] As the glitzy FTA media machine came to town, many longtime coffeehouse organizers felt pushed aside.[70]

Despite these signs of division, the FTA tour represented an important moment in the history of military resistance during the Vietnam War. Thousands of dissident soldiers were able to get a sense of their numbers, as performances were invariably packed beyond capacity, disregarding significant official and unofficial intimidation. The show's central objective—to raise public awareness of the existence of GI dissent—was seemingly accomplished, with major coverage of the FTA show appearing in the *New York Times*, the *Los Angeles Times*, and *Life* and on the three major American television networks. Jane Fonda, who had become a lightning rod for political controversy and media attention, helped direct some of that mainstream attention onto the thousands of GIs who showed up at FTA performances, providing visual evidence of the Vietnam War's unpopularity among a significant number of American soldiers. Even the FBI, in reports from undercover agents present at coffeehouse shows, somewhat begrudgingly acknowledged that Fonda's FTA show struck a chord with the crowd of active-duty GIs: "Throughout the political and military-oriented entertainment there was continuous, spontaneous and interrupting applause. The audience was captivated."[71]

THE OLEO STRUT RISES AND FALLS

The FTA show's successful tour of America's military towns brought a great deal of attention to the GI coffeehouse network, and the coffeehouses themselves enjoyed a significant rise in the number of GIs and civilians coming through the doors. However, the excitement generated by the show masked the network's tenuous position in the military towns occupied by the coffeehouses. In many locations, the FTA show staff discovered coffeehouse projects that were teetering at the edge of survival. At the Oleo Strut in Killeen, Texas, for example, organizers were facing a growing set of political, financial, and personal crises. In the spring of 1970, the staff had decided to be more open about the coffeehouse's radical politics, creating educational programs on Marxism that cast the GI movement as part of a worldwide revolution of the working class. The Oleo Strut was transformed from a coffeehouse to a "movement center," a space that was exclusively reserved for political activity. In an attempt to express an anticapitalist ethos, the staff stopped selling coffee and pastries and replaced the small "head shop" in the back of the store with tables of radical literature.

Part of the motivation for the change was, ironically enough, financial. Even at the peak of its popularity, the coffeehouse never made enough money to support its staff, who lived collectively in a small rented house. By closing down the operation of the Oleo Strut as a money-making enterprise, the staff hoped to free up time for part-time jobs in Killeen to support themselves and their political work. However, as they soon discovered, jobs in Killeen were scarce and low-paying, and by the end of the summer several staff members had dropped out of the project completely and left town, while the remaining few (among them Josh Gould, Jay Lockard, Terry Davis, and David Zeiger) were increasingly demoralized and financially challenged.[72] Compounding these problems, in September the Oleo Strut was subjected to an IRS investigation that demanded its owners produce two years of detailed financial records. Since the coffeehouse's records were in total disarray, the project took months to complete, and the coffeehouse was shuttered as the staff sorted through the mess of paperwork.[73]

The attempt to convert the Oleo Strut into a radical political movement center proved disastrous. As staff member David Zeiger put it, "In a sense, the Strut was being turned into a place that only a communist could want to have anything to do with, and as such it was on a road that was doomed to failure."[74] By eliminating most of the cultural elements that had first attracted customers, the coffeehouse unintentionally sabotaged its ability to reach large numbers of people. Gone were the rock posters and records, cheap espresso, and psychedelic atmosphere, replaced with ill-attended nightly political education programs. The only things passing as entertainment during this period were film screenings of political documentaries, intended to promote discussion and activism.[75]

By November 1970, the Oleo Strut's remaining staff members were broke, demoralized, and uncertain of the coffeehouse's future in Killeen. They drafted and sent a letter to the USSF, summarizing the coffeehouse's financial troubles and describing the bleak state of the GI movement at Fort Hood: "During this time . . . [with] the situation on Ft. Hood among those guys who were still active (which due to ETS's, transfers, and the stockade, and lack of active support from the coffeehouse had dwindled to about five guys), we more or less decided that the next couple of months would be spent trying to rebuild ourselves and the struggle on base."[76] In order to move forward as an effective tool for political organization in Killeen, the staff argued, the coffeehouse needed a permanent source of income and a coherent new political strategy. The letter paints a picture of the Oleo Strut struggling to survive.

Despite its generally pessimistic tone, the November 1970 letter also indicates that the activists at the Oleo Strut were learning from their mistakes and arriving at some important conclusions about the possibilities of their endeavor in Killeen. After a period of uncertainty as to whether the coffeehouse was a moneymaking enterprise or a political movement center, pragmatism led them to decide that it could be both. They acknowledged the necessity of a "restaurant end of things" to support their political work and help get their message to a larger number of Fort Hood soldiers: "In some ways we are going to do some back-stepping towards the days of a less political honest-to-john coffeehouse in order to make the place more popular and raise ourselves from the dead somewhat; like bands on the weekends, more comfort, and a bigger thing with the counter sales."[77] The Oleo Strut staff concluded by the late fall of 1970 that the coffeehouse needed to bring back the element of fun and entertainment that had attracted GIs in the first place. As Zeiger put it, "What's the use of a movement center if you don't even have a movement?"[78]

The Oleo Strut's new plan of action required significant funding to pay overdue bills and to make the necessary physical changes to the coffeehouse. As it happened, a new USSF office had opened in Cambridge, Massachusetts, that fall and had begun aggressively fund-raising with some success. The office started sending out vital movement information in the form of newsletters and, more important, monthly stipends to the GI coffeehouse projects. By the end of 1970, the Oleo Strut was beginning to experience a financial turnaround. In December, Jane Fonda returned to the Killeen area to help raise money for the coffeehouse, speaking at three area colleges and donating proceeds from the events. With the combined income from Fonda's appearances and a series of "emergency fund-raisers" at the coffeehouse, the Oleo Strut was in a position to enact its new strategy in the first months of 1971.

The reinvention of the Oleo Strut consisted of several changes and additions, all based on one newly clarified mission: to draw crowds, turn a profit, and help build the GI movement at Fort Hood. The first major change was the creation of a political bookstore in the back of the Oleo Strut. The bookstore was intended to answer the particular demand of black GIs, who at the time were organizing reading groups on post to discuss radical literature. A letter to the USSF in February reported, "We see the bookstore as an economic venture with an important political usefulness. We believe there's a strong political need for a broad range of revolutionary books that are easily accessible to GIs." The store also featured a counter selling a variety of small items like beaded jewelry, records, and postcards. The staff members, who considered themselves anticapitalists, were disappointed in having to engage in the "business" of running the coffeehouse but reconciled their distaste with the desperate financial times they faced: "It's quite a contradiction to our politics, to become a capitalist business and all, but it's a necessary one. If we can do this then we would only need enough regular money to keep the paper going, pay for the cost of literature and actions, and pay the staff bills (food and house)."[79]

By far the most successful element of the Oleo Strut's new strategy was a renewed focus on live entertainment, most often in the form of rock bands imported from nearby Austin's popular music scene. As the Oleo Strut became known as a hip place to see live music, the coffeehouse began regularly filling up with GIs and other locals. On performance nights, it was not uncommon to see more than 100 Fort Hood soldiers packed into the Oleo Strut. A staff member recalls that "almost overnight, the Strut became just about the most popular place in town."[80]

But the Oleo Strut's momentum was not to last. The discharge of influential GI activist Wes Williams, who left the army and returned to Oakland, left a vacuum of political leadership at Fort Hood, and activism once again slowed considerably at the end of 1971. The Strut again confronted declining morale and lower overall interest in political work among GIs on post. The fragile racial unity that had been created around issues like riot control and the "Free Harvey and Priest" campaign in the past proved unsustainable. By the time the coffeehouse began planning for the 1972 Armed Farces Day event, the People's Justice Committee had separated completely from the coffeehouse and the white GIs who made up the Fort Hood United Front. The racial animosity that had been previously overcome, if only tenuously, began to seriously erode the possibility of further racial cooperation within Fort Hood's GI movement. At the Oleo Strut, staff members faced a now-familiar set of problems: a stagnant political situation accompanied by bitter infighting and persistent financial difficulties. The coffeehouse's ability to remain open in Killeen was once again in question.[81]

As the months wore on in 1972, antiwar activism in Killeen came to a near standstill. The Oleo Strut staff attempted to regroup, but the drop-off in interest had little to do with the operation of the coffeehouses: national events were rapidly changing the landscape of political possibilities for the antiwar movement. Richard Nixon's Vietnamization strategy had already pulled 400,000 combat troops from Vietnam by the end of 1971, effectively ending the ground war and drastically shifting operations at American military bases around the world.[82] At Fort Hood, the immediate threat of being sent to Vietnam, which had provided a real sense of urgency to the local GI movement, was suddenly gone, and the activists at the Oleo Strut found themselves in a consistently empty coffeehouse. Zeiger recalled, "There was an almost instantaneous shift in the mood at Fort Hood; suddenly, there was just no one around."[83] While the Strut staff was still committed to continued antiwar activism, with the onset of Vietnamization the war was "winding down" in the minds of many Americans, including GIs at Fort Hood, and the coffeehouse project was unable to sustain the political and cultural energy it had created so effectively in the past. The Oleo Strut finally closed its doors, permanently, in the summer of 1972.

STAYING POWER: THE SHELTER HALF SOLDIERS ON

For a number of reasons, the Shelter Half coffeehouse in Tacoma, Washington, managed to last much longer than the Oleo Strut. The controversy and publicity surrounding the Shelter Half's threatened "off limits" designation in early 1970 helped establish the coffeehouse as a fixture of the region's left-wing community; it survived as an institution for several years after most other GI coffeehouse projects in military towns around the country had closed their doors. The coffeehouse undoubtedly benefited from a strong network of local radical organizations, as well as a surrounding community that was notably more accommodating than many other military towns around the country. But this long-term endurance can also be explained by the coffeehouse's conscious adaptation to changing political circumstances, both in terms of the Vietnam War itself and in the material conditions of military life at the Seattle-Tacoma area's numerous bases. As the Shelter Half made the transition from a specifically antiwar, military-oriented establishment to a more broad-based community-organizing center, it remained a consistent source of support for military activism during a period of rapid transition. Recognizing the increased involvement of the U.S. Air Force and U.S. Navy in the operation of the war, civilian organizers at the Shelter Half began to consciously orient their support activities toward these more active, non-army bases.[84]

Although by 1970 the Fort Lewis army post was playing a smaller and smaller role in the actual operation of the Vietnam War, its prominent position in the army's restructuring process ensured that institutions like the Shelter Half coffeehouse would remain in demand. One civilian organizer later explained, "We have seen that changes in U.S. military strategy have created an even greater demand than ever for [our] work."[85] To activists at the Shelter Half, the army's program of conversion from a draft system to the modern "all-volunteer force" served only to exacerbate the problems already faced by GIs. Perhaps most of all, as the VOLAR experiment came to Fort Lewis (one of three domestic posts chosen as test cases), coffeehouse organizers realized that antiwar demonstrations no longer constituted the main thrust of their activism and that their support services could be more effectively directed toward the new issues raised by the army's transition to an all-volunteer system.[86]

During the army's transition, many GI movement projects focused on providing military counseling services. Military counseling by civilians had been an important part of the antiwar movement since the beginnings of campus antiwar activism in 1964. Taking a cue from pacifist organizations that had been organizing around draft resistance and conscientious objector issues on college campuses since World War I, Students for a Democratic Society had opened off-campus draft counseling centers near universities throughout the country.⁸⁷ Later, at GI coffeehouses, antiwar activists converted the counseling strategy to suit the needs of active-duty soldiers seeking advice and information from sources other than military authorities. The service focused mainly on helping soldiers exit the military by filing for conscientious objector status but at various coffeehouses also grew to include legal counseling, help with psychological issues, and assistance in receiving health care. Coffeehouses also encouraged and hosted GI "rap groups," in which dissident soldiers could discuss their problems in a sympathetic environment. All of the different types of counseling services developed at antiwar GI coffeehouses turned a spotlight on the specific difficulties of military service, laying the foundation for future campaigns aimed at addressing persistent problems like post-traumatic stress disorder, access to health care for veterans, and obtaining honorable discharges.⁸⁸

The civilian wing's renewed focus on counseling was embodied most fully by the Pacific Counseling Service (PCS), a network of activists and lawyers created in 1969 to serve the country's West Coast and Pacific military bases. The PCS became an important force in the evolving focus of military-related civilian activism, creating a model that favored counseling and education over direct antiwar activism. The organization ultimately helped build a bridge from the New Left–style antiwar demonstrations of the late 1960s to the more legally centered GI support functions taken on by the movement as the war began to fade from public attention.⁸⁹

In the spring of 1970, representatives from the PCS met with organizers at the Shelter Half, beginning a relationship that sustained a constant presence in the area for nearly four years. The PCS ran most of its operations from the coffeehouse, including the production of a number of newspapers and publications. *Fed Up!* in particular promoted a more overt solidarity with working-class interests, especially as GIs were expressing heightened identification with labor struggles outside of the military. In early 1971, Cesar Chavez's lettuce boycott, initiated in California, became a rallying cry for activist soldiers around the country when the Department of Defense tripled its order of nonunion lettuce in a clear attempt to break the boycott.⁹⁰ *Fed Up!* and other GI papers publicized the lettuce issue and connected the exploitation and inequality experienced by agricultural workers to their own struggles against military injustice.

Organizers from the PCS, along with groups from bases around the Seattle-Tacoma region, played a central role in promoting the heightened cross-movement identification among GIs and American labor. This strategy corresponded with the military's experiments with an all-volunteer force, which, as many activists pointed out, would serve only to make the burden of military service on the working class even more pronounced. The GI Alliance, a Seattle-based organization of veterans and active-duty soldiers who met frequently at the Shelter Half, stressed the importance of working-class consciousness as the military shifted to a more economically driven system of employment: "GIs, especially in the Army, have always been predominantly from working class backgrounds. This will become increasingly true as the military moves away from the draft system. We feel that our task in the GI movement is to forge deep links between GIs and their class brothers and sisters, promote working class consciousness among GIs, and draw a clear line between them ... and their class enemies. ... As GIs begin to move in active opposition to the military, a working class outlook will be crucial in terms of building the understanding that the entire capitalist system is their enemy, not just their particular branch of service."[91]

The 1971 lettuce boycott was just one example of the GI movement's stronger connection to labor struggles in the early years of the 1970s. This connection was most powerful along the West Coast in general and specifically at Fort Lewis in Tacoma, where strong local labor organizations complemented the efforts of civilians at the Shelter Half in forging links between different wings of progressive activism. During the first few months of 1971, a constant picket line of service members and civilians distributed literature about the lettuce issue outside Fort Lewis's gates on a near-daily basis,[92] and in ensuing years soldiers from both Fort Lewis and McChord Air Force Base participated in support of union strikes involving Farah Manufacturing Company and several canneries in California.[93]

As the GI movement expanded its activities in the 1970s, its planners found themselves dealing with a host of new issues associated with the end of the war and the transition to an all-volunteer force. One more prominent issue was the increased presence of women in the military, which brought unexpected but not unfamiliar challenges to civilian and GI activists accustomed to confronting unequal, unjust working conditions.[94] From the beginning of the VOLAR experiment, organizers at the Shelter Half coffeehouse published pamphlets and articles in GI papers that pointed out the rising struggle for women's rights in the military. "Another [difficult] aspect of VOLAR," one pamphlet noted, "is the increased recruitment of women to fulfill any of the more menial and clerical jobs once performed by men. By 1976 the Pentagon plans to triple the number of women in uniform. But the military holds similar contradictions for women as for Blacks and other minorities. Although a few reforms have been made in order to allow women to occupy certain jobs, women continue to occupy an expressly inferior position in the military."[95] The efforts of the PCS and other GI organizers to increase awareness of gender issues in the military presaged the continued efforts, in later decades, to address harassment, sexual violence, and other forms of injustice experienced by women in the armed forces.[96]

Spreading awareness about important issues facing soldiers, mainly through articles in the underground press, was just one part of the support system developed at the Shelter Half coffeehouse as VOLAR came to the Tacoma area. Beyond these publicity efforts, the coffeehouse delivered free legal advice and, when necessary, representation to GIs in need. Legal services were offered most often by PCS lawyers who, according to a report distributed to national GI organizers, "provide servicemen and women with counseling and reference materials on GI rights, dependent rights, discharge policies, legal defense, and ways to file grievances and submit petitions. Much of the legal counseling deals with redress of grievances for manifestations of military repression such as illegal imprisonment, bad living and working conditions, and beatings in the brig."[97] By providing practical, material assistance to soldiers engaged in a variety of disputes, the services offered at the Shelter Half aimed to ameliorate some of the major points of dissatisfaction among GIs in a transitioning military.[98]

In September 1971, after battling with landlords over the coffeehouse's lease, the Shelter Half moved to a different building at 1902 Tacoma Avenue. The new location was much farther toward the north end of the city, placing it closer to McChord Air Force Base. Greater proximity to McChord seemed like a logical step to the Shelter Half's owners, who recognized that the momentum for antiwar organizing and other GI movement activities was shifting quickly to the air force and navy. From its second location, the Shelter Half became involved in a series of important resistance campaigns during the Vietnam War's final years. In May 1972, the coffeehouse provided publicity and support for "Project Air War," the first large-scale antiwar demonstration by airmen at McChord in the base's history.[99]

The Shelter Half's later period was also marked by a continued broadening of the regional GI movement, with organizers increasingly turning their attention to issues of community development and employment conditions. In late 1971, coffeehouse staff and activists from the GI Alliance launched a campaign to improve off-base housing conditions for GIs and their families, focusing specifically on the tiny, economically ravaged community of Tillicum, just outside Fort Lewis's main gates. Civilian organizers helped form the Tillicum Tenants' Committee, which pressured landlords through public demonstrations, leafleting, and the publication of articles exposing landlord abuse in both the *Lewis-McChord Free Press* and the committee's own newsletter, the *Tillicum News and World Report*.[100] In the spring of 1972, military officials responded to the controversy, and the Fort Lewis housing referral office began making significant improvements and ceased working with the realty offices singled out by GI organizers. The Shelter Half–sponsored effort to secure more equitable housing conditions in Tacoma reflected the changing nature of military service, which created more permanent off-base residents in need of housing for themselves and their families. By lending its support to the housing struggle, the coffeehouse signaled that its services were not limited to antiwar activism. In its later years the coffeehouse also participated in several other GI-led campaigns to improve the community, which often targeted stores and car dealerships for overcharging and otherwise exploiting naive young soldiers.[101]

The Shelter Half coffeehouse remained open in Tacoma until the summer of 1974, years after virtually every other civilian-sponsored GI project had disappeared. The coffeehouse had transformed from a psychedelic refuge for war-weary local GIs to a robust community-organizing center designed to ease the difficulties of the postwar transition to an all-volunteer force. The Shelter Half's success was made possible by the strong antiwar and radical community that existed in and around Seattle, Tacoma, and the Pacific Northwest, which helped sustain the coffeehouse and provided a constant stream of material support and activist energy. In 1974 the coffeehouse was still hosting popular free dinners on Sunday (a remnant of the New Left's communal impulses), along with daily "fifty-cent lunches" designed to serve Tacoma's low-income community. Over the course of six years, the Shelter Half went from a "GI coffeehouse" born out of the chaos of the Vietnam War to a resource center focused on a wide variety of local issues.[102]

Throughout its various phases, though, the Shelter Half directed a consistent radical voice toward local military affairs, raising concerns about life in the armed forces that continue to resonate in the twenty-first century. Perhaps most presciently, the Shelter Half regularly called attention to the complicated dynamics of gender and sexuality present in a post-1960s military. While nearly every GI coffeehouse around the country expressed some level of political feminism, the Shelter Half staff took its gender orientation to another level. In addition to leading groundbreaking campaigns focused on women in the armed forces, staff members at the Shelter Half also worked to raise awareness about the treatment of gays in the military. During the coffeehouse's final years, a gay male staff member wrote a series of articles for the *Lewis-McChord Free Press* that argued for drastic changes to official military policy regarding homosexuality and predicted that the fight for gay rights would become a critical component of future progressive efforts aimed at the armed forces.[103]

Though the Shelter Half project, along with the GI movement itself, eventually faded as the Vietnam War came to an end, its history reflects the lasting appeal of Fred Gardner's original GI coffeehouse model, which was flexible enough to survive the drastic political shifts that marked the early 1970s. Even after the Vietnam War no longer constituted the major focus of GI and activist concern, the coffeehouse was still providing a source of comfort and support for troubled soldiers. Aided immeasurably by a strong surrounding community of radical activists, the Shelter Half, like other GI coffeehouses throughout the Vietnam era, helped shine a light on the problems experienced by soldiers stationed at bases around the country and foreshadowed some of the central issues of American military life that would be faced by future generations.

Epilogue

Support Our Troops

When Fred Gardner and Donna Mickleson opened the doors of the nation's first GI coffeehouse, the UFO, in Columbia, South Carolina, in 1967, the idea inspired the creation of a whole network of coffeehouses and similar projects near military bases throughout the country. During the relatively brief time that these antiwar coffeehouses dotted the American landscape, they brought the civilian antiwar movement in direct contact with U.S. soldiers and in the process became potent symbols of a significant crisis for both the military and the nation itself. The Vietnam War had a dramatic impact on the American armed forces, and nothing demonstrated this impact more sharply than the rise of the antiwar GI movement, which created a set of institutions and resistance activities that sought to organize soldiers' anger toward the unpopular and devastating war.

The decades since the end of the Vietnam War have not witnessed a rebirth of a GI movement as profound as the one that shook the U.S. Army in the 1960s and 1970s. As wars in the Middle East take a heavy toll on American soldiers in the post-9/11 era, however, a number of antiwar GI support projects have appeared throughout the country. In the tradition of the Vietnam-era GI coffeehouse network, these new activists have created a loosely connected set of GI coffeehouses and resource centers in the same military towns that hosted these establishments at a different point in history. Places like Under the Hood Café in Killeen, Texas; Coffee Strong in Lakewood, Washington (near Joint Base Lewis-McChord); and Norfolk Offbase in Norfolk, Virginia (near Norfolk Naval Base, the largest naval base in the world), provide soldiers with an alternative set of spaces designed to address the issues faced by twenty-first-century American soldiers and veterans.[1] Rather than envision themselves as providing support for an antiwar rebellion in the armed forces, as the original coffeehouse organizers once did, these new GI coffeehouses and military support organizations focus instead on offering alternative routes through which soldiers can access help with specific issues related to their military service.

The largest of these support organizations is the GI Rights Network, a coalition of nonprofit and nongovernmental organizations formed in 1994 by the Central Committee for Conscientious Objectors.[2] Offering free, confidential information for military service members, veterans, and their families, the network operates a national hotline and website with a particular focus on discharges and filing grievances. Like the GI coffeehouse network of the Vietnam era, the GI Rights Network is supported by a wide range of individuals and institutions, including veterans' organizations like Iraq Veterans Against the War and the National Veterans Legal Services Program, organizations specializing in abuse and trauma like the Suicide Prevention Hotline and the National Sexual Assault Hotline, women's organizations like the National Women Veterans United and the Service Women's Action Network, and antiwar/antiracism groups like the War Resisters League and the National Network Opposing Militarization of Youth.

Organizations like the GI Rights Network differ from large government-chartered charities like the Wounded Warrior Project, a multimillion-dollar veterans service organization for soldiers injured in war, and Operation Homefront, which offers emergency support services to soldiers and veterans. These groups are among a number of officially sanctioned support organizations that have arisen since September 11, 2001. Mainstream charities like the Wounded Warrior Project are distinct from left-oriented organizations like the current crop of GI coffeehouses, which offer support for soldiers independent of official military channels, in the context of an antiwar political framework. These GI support organizations follow the model of left outreach to soldiers that reached its fullest expression during the Vietnam War, combining practical and material support within a larger critique of American war policy. More important, though, they offer soldiers a support network that exists outside of the military's institutional structures. This outside role is especially critical when dealing with sensitive issues like sexual abuse, drug and alcohol addiction, gender- and race-based harassment, psychological trauma, and a host of other problems faced by modern GIs.

Creating spaces where soldiers can access information and resources, off the record and away from military administration, has evolved into one of the most critical functions performed by activist GI projects. While a large number and variety of charitable groups aim to help American soldiers deal with the fallout of war, the Left's contribution remains a prominent and unique one. Recognizing the role that antiwar activists have played, and continue to play, in offering GI support disrupts the popular image of soldiers and left activists pitted against one another, an idea that has often played out politically through the concept of "support."

In the decades since the Vietnam War came to an end, the notion of "supporting our troops" took on a powerful place in public discourse. Along with the start of the Gulf War in 1990, conservative politicians, pundits, and citizens popularized the slogan "Support Our Troops" in an attempt to make up for the perceived disrespect directed at soldiers in the Vietnam era. The historical revisionism embedded in the phrase conflates respect for soldiers with support for war policy and dissent with contempt for the troops. In this reactionary version of history, in times of war the American Left stands on the sidelines, jeering and spitting at soldiers, while patriotic Americans offer nothing but their steadfast "support" for our brave troops. But the history of the GI coffeehouse network of the Vietnam years, along with the many associated movements and institutions created by the Left in the ensuing decades, contradicts this dominant narrative. Since the 1960s, while conservatives engaged in a concerted effort to own the "Support Our Troops" brand, activists on the Left have been building networks and organizations that, in both practical and material terms, accomplish just that. Drawing inspiration from the GI coffeehouses that first dotted the landscape in the 1960s and 1970s, peace activists in the twenty-first century continue to create dynamic institutions to counter the heavy toll of war and militarism felt by the men and women of the nation's armed forces.

Of course, the culture and politics that surround activist-operated GI support projects, including GI coffeehouses, have shifted dramatically since the Vietnam War era. Organizers at the Different Drummer Café, a GI coffeehouse that opened near the Fort Drum army post in upstate New York in 2007, struggled to come to terms with how changes in military service since Vietnam have affected their work. After the coffeehouse officially closed in 2009, its owner and operator, Tod Ensign, reflected on these changes:

> We carefully compared the US military during Vietnam to the present "all volunteer" force. The most obvious difference is that after conscription was ended in 1973, our military no longer represented a

cross-section of American society. One third of the troops in Vietnam were draftees with another third being "draft induced" volunteers. Today, virtually all enlisted soldiers are from working class or poor families. Secondly, they receive pay and bonuses which in most cases are competitive or superior to what they would earn in civilian jobs. During Vietnam, many soldiers earned $120 a month, lived in crowded barracks and took their meals in dismal chow halls. Only a few were married or owned a car. Today, over half of all Army soldiers are married and most of these are also parents. You won't find many soldiers today who don't own a cell phone, a lap top computer as well as a car or a truck. They use this mobility to escape the base whenever possible, often travelling hundreds of miles.[3]

As Ensign points out, the often dismal conditions faced by American soldiers during the Vietnam War inadvertently contributed to and helped build a movement of soldiers against war. But, as he also explains, the wars in Iraq and Afghanistan have, in many ways, demanded more sacrifice from GIs than ever before.

I believe that combat soldiers from these current wars suffer more stress and mental dysfunction than even those who served in Vietnam. Their rates for PTSD, depression and suicide so far confirm this conclusion. This is partly because they are forced to endure multiple deployments in combat zones where the tension and danger never lets up. However, I've learned in my forty years of activism that the level of oppression someone experiences is not predictive of whether he or she will fight back or instead seek escape through self-destructive behaviors.[4]

While the Different Drummer Cafe, like Fred Gardner's original GI coffeehouse network, enjoyed only a brief existence, other GI organizers and activists have carried on the coffeehouse tradition. Navigating a very different political and cultural landscape from the one in which the coffeehouse organizers of the 1960s and 1970s first operated, the latest group of GI support projects focus their efforts on addressing the specific issues faced by soldiers in today's U.S. military. With the men and women of the nation's armed services continuing to bear the brunt of America's seemingly endless military engagements, these projects build on the legacy of GI support modeled by the GI coffeehouse network of the Vietnam War era, working to create places where soldiers can find resources and support for the serious issues they face.[5]

Notes

Introduction

1. Lewis, *Hard Hats, Hippies, and Hawks*, 35–45. Lewis profiles a number of canonical works, including Gitlin, *Sixties*; Miller, *Democracy Is in the Streets*; Albert and Albert, *Sixties Papers*; and Sayres et al., *60s without Apology*.
2. See Lembke, *Spitting Image*.
3. Small, *Give Peace a Chance*, 96.
4. Cortright, *Soldiers in Revolt*, 12–13.
5. Ibid., 201–7.
6. Chambers, *Oxford Companion to American Military History*.
7. Cortright, *Soldiers in Revolt*, 40.
8. Bailey, *America's Army*, 130–71.
9. "Return to Fort Dix," *Shakedown*, vol. 2, no. 2, May 1971, Underground GI Newspapers, The Sixties Project digital archives.
10. *GI News and Discussion Bulletin*, no. 8, August 1971; "Report from the Fort Bragg Collective (Haymarket Square Coffeehouse)," box 1, folder "Project Description (Internal)," Cortright Papers, Swarthmore College Peace Collection; McCallum, *Yes to the Troops*, 127–34.
11. Goldman, "Changing Role of Women in the Armed Forces." See also Herbert, *Camouflage Isn't Only for Combat*.
12. William Yardley, "Andy Stapp, Who Tried to Unionize the Military, Dies at 70," *New York Times*, September 14, 2014.
13. Halstead, *Out Now!*
14. Lutz, *Homefront*, 146.
15. Enke, *Finding the Movement*, 2.
16. Appy, *Working Class War*, 51.

Chapter 1

1. "Frederick H. Gardner Writer Profile," *Harvard Crimson* website, http://www.thecrimson.com/writer/5771/Frederick_H._Gardner/, accessed July 11, 2010. The site contains an archive of all of Gardner's writings from 1961 to 1963.
2. Fred Gardner, interview by author, January 15, 2011.
3. Fred Gardner, "Hollywood Confidential, Part I," *Vietnam Generation Journal and Newsletter*, vol. 3, no. 3, November 1991, 36.
4. Heinl, "Collapse of the Armed Forces," 35.
5. Hunt, *Turning*, 5–6, 10–12.
6. Gardner, "Hollywood Confidential, Part I," 37.
7. Appy, *Working Class War*, 51. "Draft-motivated volunteers" refers to those soldiers who joined the armed forces voluntarily with the (oftentimes erroneous) perception that, by volunteering, they would obtain more favorable terms of service, such as choice of branch and avoidance of combat, than if they waited to be drafted.
8. Cortright, *Soldiers in Revolt*, 52; "Antiwar Sentiment is Deep at Ft. Jackson Army Base," *Militant*, March 18, 1968.
9. Myers, *Black, White, and Olive Drab*, 189–204. For more on the Levy case, see Andrew Kopkind, "The Trial of Captain Levy," *New York Review of Books*, April 11, 1968; Ira Glasser, "Justice and Captain Levy," *Columbia Forum*, Spring 1969, 46–49; and Douglas E. Kneeland, "War Stirs GI Dissent," *New York Times*, June 21, 1970.
10. Fred Gardner, "Hollywood Confidential, Part II," *Vietnam Generation Journal and Newsletter*, vol. 3, no. 3, November 1991, 36–40. Gardner mentions his admiration for Levy, specifically for his refusal to serve and the resulting Fort Jackson court-martial.
11. Moore, *Columbia and Richland County*, 359.
12. Ibid.
13. Ibid., 393.
14. Fred Gardner, "Case Study in Opportunism: The GI Movement," *Second Page Supplement*, October 1971, 2.
15. Ibid., 2.
16. Ibid., 2–4.
17. Ibid.
18. Gardner, "Hollywood Confidential, Part I," 4.
19. Ibid., 5.
20. McAninch, "UFO," 1.
21. Quoted in ibid., 2.
22. Cortright, *Soldiers in Revolt*, 53.
23. Donald Janson, "Antiwar Coffeehouses Delight G.I.'s but Not Army," *New York Times*, August 12, 1968.
24. Quoted in ibid. The "All America City Award" is a program, still in existence, begun in 1949, sponsored by the National Civic League. The award is "the oldest community recognition program in the nation . . . [and] recognizes communities whose citizens work together to identify and tackle community-wide challenges and achieve uncommon results." Smith, *Fayetteville, North Carolina*, 137.
25. Janson, "Antiwar Coffeehouses Delight G.I.'s but Not Army."

26. Schulman, *The Seventies*, 112.
27. Myers, *Black, White, and Olive Drab*, 3.
28. "No Praying on the Chapel Steps," *Vietnam GI*, April 1968, 8.
29. Gardner, "Case Study in Opportunism," 2–3.
30. "No Praying on the Chapel Steps," 8.
31. Ibid.
32. "Two at Ft. Jackson May Face Charges," *The State*, February 22, 1968; "Two at Fort Jackson Court-Martial over War Doubts," *New York Times*, February 22, 1968, 10; Douglas Robinson, "Leaflets Bombard Fort Jackson G.I.'s Off-Post," *New York Times*, February 24, 1968; "Two GIs Face Trial for 'Pray-In' on War," *Militant*, February 26, 1968, 1.
33. Mailer's *Armies of the Night* undoubtedly provides the most compelling account of the 1967 March on the Pentagon, though less historically "novelized" narratives can be found in Gitlin, *Sixties*, 254–55, and in Halstead, *Out Now!*, 336–40.
34. Gardner, "Hollywood Confidential, Part I," 4.
35. "USOs for Peace are Coming," *Ally*, no. 5 (June 1968), 3, Tamiment Library, New York University.
36. United States, Congress, House, Committee on Internal Security, *Subversive Involvement*, part 2, 2667.
37. Gardner, "Case Study in Opportunism," 4.
38. The United States Servicemen's Fund Records, located in the archives of the Wisconsin Historical Society, contains newsletters, correspondence, and pamphlets that demonstrate the powerful role the organization played in supporting the coffeehouse and GI movements.
39. "Introduction to USSF," *About Face! The U.S. Servicemen's Fund Newsletter* 2, no. 4 (January 1969), Underground GI Newspapers, The Sixties Project digital archives.
40. United States, Congress, House, Committee on Internal Security, *Subversive Involvement*, part 2, 2667.
41. Gardner, "Hollywood Confidential, Part II."
42. The Uniform Code of Military Justice, Article 88, part of a section of articles dealing with dissent, reads: "Any commissioned officer who uses contemptuous words against the President, the Vice President, Congress, the Secretary of Defense, the Secretary of a military department, the Secretary of Transportation, or the Governor or legislature of any State, Territory, Commonwealth, or possession in which he is on duty or present shall be punished as a court-martial may direct." The final article of the code's "punitive" section, Article 134, reads: "Though not specifically mentioned in this chapter, all disorders and neglects to the prejudice of good order and discipline in the armed forces, all conduct of a nature to bring discredit upon the armed forces, and crimes and offenses not capital, of which persons subject to this chapter may be guilty, shall be taken cognizance of by a general, special, or summary court-martial, according to the nature and degree of the offense, and shall be punished at the discretion of that court." Cheryl Rodewig, "Social Media Misuse Punishable Under UCMJ," February 9, 2012. https://www.army.mil/article/73367/Social_media_misuse_punishable_under_UCMJ/.
43. John Rechy, "Conduct Unbecoming: Lieutenant on the Peace Line," *Nation*, February 21, 1966, 204–8; Lynd, *We Won't Go*, 181–202.

44. Cortright, *Soldiers in Revolt*, 51.
45. Ibid., 53–55.
46. Paul Eberle, "Dr. Levy on GI Repression," *Los Angeles Free Press*, May 15, 1970.
47. United States Servicemen's Fund, Organizational Letter, Fall 1969, GI Movement Archive, Swarthmore College Peace Collection.
48. Ibid.
49. "Introduction to USSF," *About Face! United States Servicemen's Fund Newsletter* 2, no. 4 (January 1969), Underground GI Newspapers, The Sixties Project digital archives.
50. Ibid.
51. Josh Gould, telephone interview by author, January 25, 2010.
52. Bell County Historical Commission, *Story of Bell County*, 34.
53. Duncan, *Killeen*, 94.
54. Ibid.; Bell County Historical Commission, *Story of Bell County*, 46–49.
55. Duncan, *Killeen*, 94.
56. "Fort Hood GI Haven," *Space City News*, Fall 1970.
57. Zeiger, *History of the Oleo Strut Coffeehouse*, 3.
58. Dane, "Oleo Strut."
59. Cortright, *Soldiers in Revolt*, 56.
60. "The Big Smear," editorial comment, *Killeen (Tex.) Daily Herald*, July 25, 1968.
61. Dane, "Oleo Strut." Nicholas von Hoffman's reporting on Fort Hood in the *Washington Post* throughout 1968 also details the post's intense explosion of drug use and countercultural expression among soldiers, which included a prolonged battle over allowable hair length.
62. Ibid.
63. Zeiger, *History of the Oleo Strut Coffeehouse*, 2.
64. At the time, when the Killeen city police department arrested Fort Hood GIs, it regularly transferred them to the custody of military police. "Frame-up at Ft. Head," *Vietnam GI*, September 1968.
65. Lewes, *Protest and Survive*, 176.
66. Gallacci and Karabaich, *Tacoma's Waterfront*, 4–8.
67. Swarner, *Evergreen Post*, 54–55; Archie Satterfield, "Fort Lewis 'Search, Destroy Mission,'" *Seattle Times Sunday Magazine*, August 25, 1969, 28–29.
68. Swarner, *Evergreen Post*, 55; leaflet, Fort Lewis Military Museum, U.S. Army Museum System, Center of Military History.
69. Leaflet, Fort Lewis Military Museum, U.S. Army Museum System, Center of Military History, Fort Lewis, Wash.
70. "Military Pay Raise Bill Seen Benefit to Area," *Tacoma News Tribune*, April 29, 1966, A1.
71. Wallace Turner, "GI Coffeehouse under Coast Fire," *New York Times*, February 16, 1969.
72. Sale, *SDS*.
73. Isserman, *If I Had a Hammer*, 63. The Young Socialist Alliance was a Trotskyist youth group, a wing of the Socialist Workers Party in the United States. The YSA was founded in 1960 and was active in antiwar demonstrations and other forms of radical

activism through the early 1990s. See also Halstead, *Out Now!* Halstead's comprehensive history covers the group's trajectory through the 1960s and early 1970s.

74. "Statement of the University of Washington Young Socialist Alliance," March 6, 1969, SDS Papers, accession 1080–4, box 1, University of Washington, Seattle, Special Collections, Suzzallo Library.

75. Edd Jeffords, "Coffeehouse Achieves Goal of Getting People Together," *Tacoma News Tribune*, October 13, 1968.

76. Letter to Shelter Half Staff, April 21, 1969, SDS Papers, accession 1080–4, box 1, University of Washington, Seattle, Special Collections, Suzzallo Library. The GI and friend did not include their names in the letter.

77. Letter, *Counterpoint*, September 20, 1969, Underground GI Newspapers, The Sixties Project digital archives.

78. Jeffords, "Coffeehouse Achieves Goal of Getting People Together."

79. Barbara Garson, interview with author, May 7, 2011.

80. Ibid.

81. Turner, "GI Coffeehouse under Coast Fire."

Chapter 2

1. Donald Janson, "Antiwar Coffeehouses Delight G.I.'s but Not Army," *New York Times*, August 12, 1968.

2. The most detailed source on the Fort Jackson Eight case is Halstead, *GIs Speak Out against the War*. See also "Army Urged to Free 8 Protesting War," *New York Times*, April 12, 1969.

3. Douglas E. Kneeland, "War Stirs GI Dissent," *New York Times*, June 21, 1970.

4. GIs United Against the War in Vietnam, "Statement of Aims," in Halstead, *GIs Speak Out against the War*, 97.

5. Cortright, *Soldiers in Revolt*, 59–60.

6. "GI War 'Dissident' Is Army Informer," *New York Times*, April 9, 1969.

7. Ben A. Franklin, "Army Bars Trial 3 Antiwar GIs; Drops Fort Jackson Case—Discharges Are Set," *New York Times*, May 21, 1969.

8. Lewes, *Protest and Survive*, 97.

9. Halstead, *GIs Speak Out against the War*, 6.

10. "Fort Jackson GIs Win Victory!," *Dull Brass*, vol.1, no. 2, May 1969, Underground GI Newspapers Collection, Cortright Papers, Swarthmore College Peace Collection.

11. Cortright, *Soldiers in Revolt*, 59–61.

12. Halstead, *GIs Speak Out against the War*, 9.

13. John Kifner, "Thousands of U.S. Troops Mobilized for Guard Duty at Democratic Convention," *New York Times*, August 25, 1968; J. Anthony Lukas, "Chicago Is Prague," ibid., August 25, 1968. See also interview with Haywood T. "The Kid" Kirkland (Ari Sesu Merretazon) in Terry, *Bloods*, 100. In the interview, one of several conversations Terry had with black GIs who refused riot duty at Chicago, Merretazon expresses a common sentiment: "I told them I'm not going there holding no weapon in front of my brothers and sisters." "GI Black Panther Lists Motivation," *Overseas Weekly–Pacific Edition*, May 3, 1969.

14. "Remember the Fort Hood 43!," *Vietnam GI*, August 1969.

15. Ibid.
16. Zeiger, *History of the Oleo Strut Coffeehouse*, 3.
17. Kifner, "Thousands of U.S. Troops Mobilized for Guard Duty at Democratic Convention."
18. "3 More Convicted in Protest at Fort," *New York Times*, September 29, 1968; Fred P. Graham, "Testing the Issue of Soldiers' Rights," ibid., March 23, 1969.
19. Josh Gould, telephone interview by author, January 25, 2010.
20. Zeiger, *History of the Oleo Strut Coffeehouse*, 3.
21. "A Report from the Oleo Strut," *New SOS News*, vol. 1, no. 4, July 1969. "EM" is a common army term meaning enlisted man (or men).
22. Allah, *In the Name of Allah*.
23. "Report from the Oleo Strut."
24. Ibid.
25. GI Civil Liberties Defense Committee, *Free Richard Chase* pamphlet, December 20, 1969, http://sirnosir.com/archives_and_resources/library/pamphlets_publications (accessed July 19, 2010).
26. "Free All Political Prisoners," *Left Face*, no. 5, January 1970, Underground GI Newspapers Collection, Cortright Papers, Swarthmore College Peace Collection.
27. Quoted in Zeiger, *History of the Oleo Strut Coffeehouse*, 7.
28. Ibid.
29. "Political Prisoner at Fort Hood," *Black Panther*, December 27, 1969; "Free Richard Chase," *GI Press Service*, vol. 1, no. 13; GI Civil Liberties Defense Committee, *Free Richard Chase* pamphlet; "Free All Political Prisoners," *Left Face*, no. 5, January 1970; "Riot Control," *Aboveground*, vol. 1, no. 6, December 1969, Underground GI Newspapers Collection, Cortright Papers, Swarthmore College Peace Collection; "No to Riot Control: GI Gets Two Years Hard Labor," *Black Panther*, January 10, 1970.
30. "Richard Chase Sentenced," *GI Press Service*, vol. 2, no. 1, January 21, 1970.
31. Zeiger, *History of the Oleo Strut Coffeehouse*, 7.
32. Oppenheimer, *American Military*, 100; "G.I. Press," *WIN*, December 1, 1969, 22–25.
33. Quoted in Stacewicz, *Winter Soldiers*, 225.
34. Ibid., 226.
35. David Zeiger, interview by author, January 5, 2010.
36. Moser, *New Winter Soldiers*, 99. The story of the shooting is recounted in detail by Dave Cline in Stacewicz, *Winter Soldiers*, 222–26. See also Seymour V. Connor and Mark Odintz, "Bell County," *Handbook of Texas Online*, http://www.tshaonline.org/handbook/online/articles/hcb06, accessed April 17, 2012. This article details the Ku Klux Klan's presence in Bell County, Texas (including Killeen), beginning during the Reconstruction period and reappearing in waves throughout the twentieth century.
37. Christopher S. Wren, "Protest in the Ranks! The Military's New Dilemma," *Look*, vol. 32, no. 21, October 15, 1968; Ben A. Franklin, "Antiwar G.I.'s and Army Head for Clash over Vietnam," *New York Times*, April 28, 1969, 22; "Exclusive! The Plot to Unionize the U.S. Army," *Esquire*, August 1968; "Extraordinary Military," *Life*, May 23, 1969.
38. Fonda, *My Life So Far*, 258.
39. Fred Gardner, "Hollywood Confidential, Part I," 35.

Notes to Pages 52–56

40. Nat Henderson, "Actress Barred from Ft. Hood," *Killeen Daily Herald*, May 12, 1970, 1.
41. Quoted in Martin Dreyer, "War and Peace at the Oleo Strut," *Houston Chronicle*, July 12, 1970.
42. Hershberger, *Jane Fonda's War*, 17.
43. Armed Forces Day was created in 1949 as a national holiday to honor all military branches, an action stemming from the unification of all the branches under the Department of Defense in the wake of World War II.
44. Zeiger, *History of the Oleo Strut Coffeehouse*, 8. The Oleo Strut staff initially did not believe it was possible to organize a large demonstration of GIs in Killeen and instead planned to offer "Nine Days in May," an alternative week of educational programs and guest speakers at the coffeehouse. As the national event approached, and it became clear that many base towns would be holding large public demonstrations, those on the staff changed their minds. On May 10, they decided to attempt to organize an Armed Farces Day parade through the center of downtown Killeen. The May 16 parade committee, composed of Oleo Strut staff and Fort Hood GIs, applied to Killeen City Hall for a parade permit and were denied, but a constitutional lawyer hired by the committee sent a letter threatening legal action that convinced the city to grant the permit.
45. Quoted in Stacewicz, *Winter Soldiers*, 225.
46. "1,000 GIs March in Killeen," *Fatigue Press*, no. 23, August 1970; "Armed Farces Day, May 20," *Off the Brass*, vol. 1, no. 3, May 1970.
47. Duncan, *Killeen*, 151.
48. "Armed Forces Day," *A Four Year Bummer*, vol. 2, no. 4, June 1970.
49. "1,000 GIs March in Killeen."
50. Zeiger interview.
51. *GI Legal Self Defense* pamphlet, Spring 1971, http://sirnosir.com/archives_and_resources/library/pamphlets_publications/gi_legal_self_defense/cover.html, accessed March 22, 2011. Originally produced by the "People's House," a GI coffeehouse and movement center in Clarksville, Tennessee, outside Fort Campbell, the pamphlet was reproduced in various forms and distributed around military bases throughout the country and overseas. In addition to relevant citations from the Uniform Code of Military Justice, the pamphlet offered GIs tips on avoiding harassment and protecting their civil liberties.
52. Jay Dorman, "The Strut Limps Along," *Houston Post*, April 12, 1971; Cortright, *Soldiers in Revolt*, 67.
53. Zeiger, *History of the Oleo Strut Coffeehouse*, 12.
54. Tom Butler, "Protest March, Rally Held in Orderly Manner," *Killeen Daily Herald*, May 16, 1971; Duncan, *Killeen*, 151.
55. Zeiger, *History of the Oleo Strut Coffeehouse*, 13.
56. "We Don't Want Your Rip Off Store," *Camp News*, vol. 2, no. 8, 1971.
57. Dave Cline, interview in the film *Sir! No Sir!* Cline's detailed description of the Tyrrell's boycott in Killeen casts the action as one of the high points of the GI movement.
58. "2 of 10 Post Bonds in Store Picketing," *Killeen Daily Herald*, June 3, 1971; "Great Lakes: MDM Wins First Round of Jewelry Store Boycott," *Camp News*, vol. 2, no. 8, 1971.

59. "Analysis: The Tyrrell's Boycott in Killeen," staff report, *GI News and Discussion Bulletin*, no. 7, July 1971. Cam Cunningham was an Austin attorney who defended the Oleo Strut's staff, as well as Fort Hood GIs, on several occasions from 1970 to 1972.

60. "Boycott in Killeen Advances," *GI News and Discussion Bulletin*, no. 6, June 1971. Farmworkers' organizations in Texas were, at the time, involved in a similar court fight challenging the constitutionality of secondary boycott laws.

61. Anderson, "GI Movement and the Response from the Brass," 110. Anderson states, "The [Tyrrell's] boycott spread to eleven bases, significantly reducing sales. The chain store ended the action by negotiating new sales procedures with GI organizations."

62. *Petition to Free Harvey and Priest*, Fort Hood United Front, http://sirnosir.com/archives_and_resources/library/pamphlets_publications/petitions/harvey_priest.html, accessed June 1, 2010.

63. Cortright, *Soldiers in Revolt*, 84. Activists chose Stillhouse Lake because groups were not required to obtain permits for picnics, barbecues, and other recreational activities.

64. Ibid.; Zeiger interview.

65. *Black Organization Grows from Hearing on Racism*, Fort Hood United Front pamphlet, Division of Rare and Manuscript Collections, Cornell University.

66. Derrick Morrison, "Black Caucus Exposes Military Racism," *Militant*, December 3, 1971.

67. Zeiger interview.

68. *Black Organization Grows from Hearing on Racism*, Fort Hood United Front pamphlet. See also "Military Race Relations Held Explosive," *New York Times*, November 18, 1971; and Honorable Louis Stokes, "Racism in the Military: A New System for Rewards and Punishment," Congressional Black Caucus Report, *Congressional Record*, 92nd Cong., 2nd sess., October 14, 1972.

69. Cortright, *Soldiers in Revolt*, 88–89.

70. Zeiger, *History of the Oleo Strut Coffeehouse*, 20–21.

71. Letter, *Counterpoint*, September 20, 1969, 4, Underground GI Newspapers, The Sixties Project digital archives.

72. United States, Congress, House, Committee on Internal Security, *Workers World Party and Its Front Organizations*, 21. The Committee on Internal Security report refers to the American Servicemen's Union as one of the (Socialist) Workers World Party's primary American front organizations. Before forming the ASU, Stapp had been court-martialed in the late 1960s for his antiwar activities. The ASU evolved into a forceful presence within the Vietnam-era GI movement before dissolving in the years after the war.

73. "Report on the March and Rally," *Counterpoint*, February 24, 1969; "Report on Antiwar Actions," ibid., April 14, 1969, Underground GI Newspapers, The Sixties Project digital archives.

74. "Report on Antiwar Actions."

75. Peck, *Uncovering the Sixties*, 12–14.

76. United States, Congress, House, Committee on Internal Security, *Investigation of Attempts to Subvert the United States Armed Services* (hereafter United States, *Investigation*), part 1, 6411.

77. Kindig, "Demilitarized Zone," 16.
78. Ibid., 18.
79. United States, *Investigation*, part 1, 6414.
80. "Woman Leads 'Invasion' at Coast's Fort Lewis," *Pittsburgh Press*, July 14, 1969; "Fort Invaders Given Warning," *Spokane Daily Chronicle*, July 14, 1969; "Peace Invaders," *Ellensburg (Wash.) Daily Record*, July 12, 1969; "Fort Lewis 'Liberation' Falls Flat; 7 Arrested," *Lodi (Calif.) News-Sentinel*, July 14, 1969.
81. "The Great Invasion," *Counterpoint*, August 7, 1969, Underground GI Newspapers, The Sixties Project digital archives; Peter Arnett, "Major Describes Move," *New York Times*, February 8, 1968. Coontz was referring to one of the most famous quotes of the Vietnam War, from an article by AP correspondent Peter Arnett. Writing about the provincial capital, Bến Tre, on February 7, 1968, Arnett reported, "'It became necessary to destroy the town to save it,' a United States major said today. He was talking about the decision by allied commanders to bomb and shell the town regardless of civilian casualties, to rout the Vietcong."
82. "The Great Invasion," *Counterpoint*, August 7, 1969, Underground GI Newspapers, The Sixties Project digital archives.
83. Staff editorial, *Fed Up!*, vol. 1, no. 1, October 13, 1969, Underground GI Newspapers, The Sixties Project digital archives.
84. Lewes, *Protest and Survive*, 46.
85. *Seattle Times*, October 21, 1969, 6.
86. Rinaldi, "The Olive-Drab Rebels," 37–38.
87. Steven V. Roberts, "17 G.I.'s Sue to Clarify Speech and Assembly Rights," *New York Times*, October 29, 1969.
88. Stapp, *Up against the Brass*, 88–90.
89. "GIs Refuse Vietnam Duty," *A Four Year Bummer*, vol. 2, no. 6, August 1970.
90. "Hands Off the Shelter Half," *Fed Up!*, vol. 1, no. 3, January 16, 1970, Underground GI Newspapers, The Sixties Project digital archives; Capt. H. W. Stauffacher, letter on behalf of Armed Forces Disciplinary Control Board, to proprietor of Shelter Half Coffeehouse, December 11, 1969, reprinted in Waterhouse and Wizard, *Turning the Guns Around*, 78–79.

Chapter 3

1. United States, Congress, House, Committee on Internal Security, *Subversive Involvement*.
2. Hunt, *David Dellinger*, 215–28. See also Sossi, *Voices of the Chicago Eight*.
3. United States, Congress, House, Committee on Internal Security, *Investigation of Attempts to Subvert the United States Armed Services* (hereafter United States, *Investigation*), part 2, 2667–68.
4. Ibid., 2681.
5. Ibid.
6. Ibid., 2673.
7. For a wider discussion of Heinl and the internal conflict concerning military policy during the later years of the Vietnam War, see Cincinnatus, *Self-Destruction*, 10.

8. United States, *Investigation*, part 2, 7080–81.

9. By 1971, HUAC, which had been in charge of the first congressional investigation of the GI coffeehouse network, had significantly diminished in power and public esteem. The stain of McCarthyism haunted the committee throughout the 1960s, and many Americans regarded the institution as a relic of an unpleasant era. Public disdain for HUAC's investigations caused the committee to change its name in 1969, removing the politically divisive term "Un-American" and rebranding itself the "Committee on Internal Security." In 1975, the House of Representatives voted to abolish the committee altogether; its functions were folded into the House Judiciary Committee. Navasky, *Naming Names*, 12–15; Staples, *Encyclopedia of Privacy*, 284.

10. United States, *Investigation*, part 2, 6382.

11. Ibid.

12. In his 1971 article, Heinl referred to the "communist" National Mobilization Committee as the coffeehouse network's main ideological supporters, despite the fact that the Mobe had disintegrated in the late 1960s.

13. Thomas Geoghegan, "By Any Other Name. Brass Tacks," *Harvard Crimson*, February 24, 1969. Geoghegan captured the wider cultural changes that undermined HUAC's authority: "In the fifties, the most effective sanction was terror. Almost any publicity from HUAC meant the 'blacklist.' Without a chance to clear his name, a witness would suddenly find himself without friends and without a job. But it is not easy to see how in 1969 a HUAC blacklist could terrorize an SDS activist. Witnesses like Jerry Rubin have openly boasted of their contempt for American institutions. A subpoena from HUAC would be unlikely to scandalize Abbie Hoffman or his friends."

14. United States, *Investigation*, part 2, 7002.

15. "Council May Use New Ordinance to Bar Coffeehouse in Muldraugh," *Louisville Courier-Journal*, September 24, 1969; Frank Ashley, "Muldraugh Coffeehouse Scene of Quiet Protest," ibid., October 16, 1969.

16. "Fact Sheet on GI Coffeehouse," *Fun Travel Adventure*, no. 16, September 1969, Tamiment Library, New York University.

17. *Fort Knox Coffeehouse Report*, supplement to USSF newsletter, December 1969.

18. Bill Peterson, "Viet Veteran Defends Coffeehouse as Muldraugh Eviction Trial Ends," *Louisville Courier-Journal*, September 26, 1969; Bill Peterson, "Exiles by Choice," ibid., September 23, 1971.

19. "Letter to the Editor," *Killeen Daily Herald*, May 18, 1971.

20. Ibid., May 23, 1971.

21. Ibid., October 28, 1971.

22. Ibid.

23. Mark Lane, "The Covered Wagon: Finding the Power to Affect our Destinies," *Helping Hand*, no. 10, May 1972, Underground GI Newspapers, The Sixties Project digital archives.

24. "The Covered Wagon," letter to the *New York Review of Books*, December 30, 1971. The letter was signed by a number of the USSF's most visible public supporters, including Noam Chomsky, Faye Dunaway, Jane Fonda, Dick Gregory, and Arthur Miller.

25. Ibid.

26. "Visit From a Former P.O.W. George Smith," *Helping Hand*, no. 8, February 1972, Underground GI Newspapers, The Sixties Project digital archives.

27. "Fort Dix Coffeehouse Bombing," USSF transcription of phone call from Leroy Townley, http://sirnosir.com/archives_and_resources/library/pamphlets_publications. Townley was a member of the Fort Dix Coffeehouse collective and a witness to the incident.

28. "Soldier Is Still Hospitalized after Bombing at Fort Dix," *New York Times*, February 17, 1970.

29. Paul Eberle, "Dr. Levy on GI Repression," *Los Angeles Free Press*, May 15, 1970.

30. Ibid.

31. Letter dated July 5, 1968, http://www.icdc.com/~paulwolf/cointelpro/director5july1968.htm, digital scan accessed July 17, 2010. For more on the counterintelligence program's specific targeting of New Left groups, see Davis, *Assault on the Left*; Jeffreys-Jones, *FBI*; and Cunningham, *There's Something Happening Here*.

32. "Politics Are Off Limits at Fort Lewis," *Black Panther*, January 17, 1970.

33. "Coffeehouse to Fight Off-Limits Designation," *Tacoma News Tribune*, December 18, 1969.

34. "Hands Off the Shelter Half," *Fed Up!*, vol. 1, no. 3, January 16, 1970, Underground GI Newspapers, The Sixties Project digital archives. Other popular Fort Lewis–area GI antiwar publications included *B Troop News* and *Lewis-McChord Free Press* (Tillicum, Wash.).

35. Cortright, *Soldiers in Revolt*, 76–77.

36. "'Trial' Finds Army Guilty," *Seattle Post-Intelligencer*, January 22, 1970; "Trial of the Army," *Fed Up!*, vol. 1, no. 4, February 26, 1970, Underground GI Newspapers, The Sixties Project digital archives.

37. *From the Shelter Half* pamphlet, February 1970, http://sirnosir.com/archives_and_resources/library/pamphlets_publications/repression/shelter_half/page1.html, accessed July 19, 2010.

38. "Coffeehouse Claims GI Held in 'Reprisal,'" *Tacoma News Tribune*, January 26, 1970.

39. "On Limits," *Fed Up!*, vol. 1, no. 4, February 26, 1970, Underground GI Newspapers, The Sixties Project digital archives.

40. Lee, "Fed Up at Fort Lewis," 21–23.

41. *From the Shelter Half.*

42. Cortright, *Soldiers in Revolt*, 174.

43. Other "identity"-based GI antiwar publications included *Black Unity* (Camp Pendleton, Calif.), and the Native American–focused *Broken Arrow* (Selfridge Air Force Base, Mich.).

44. Memorandum, Major General Kenneth G. Wickham, Adjutant General, to Commanding Generals, May 28, 1969, subj.: Guidance on Dissent, Records of the Historical Services Division Relating to Army Organizations and Operations, National Archives and Records Administration, Record Group 472, box 14, 3.

45. Ibid., 6.

46. Ibid., 4.

47. Keeney, "Resistance," 58.

48. McAninch, "UFO," 7.
49. Grose, "Voices of Southern Protest during the Vietnam War Era," 158.
50. Lee Bandy, "FBI Files Tell of Work against USC Left, UFO," *The State*, December 16, 1977, A1.
51. McAninch, "UFO," 7.
52. Giles, "Antiwar Movement in Columbia, South Carolina," 13.
53. Ibid., 12.
54. Quoted in Myers, *Black, White, and Olive Drab*, 203.
55. *The State*, August 2, 1969.
56. Transcript of testimony at 125, *State v. Hannafan*, Court of General Sessions, Indictment No. 240, Fifth Judicial Circuit of South Carolina (April 15, 1970, through April 28, 1970).
57. McAninch, "UFO," 7.
58. Ibid.
59. *The State*, January 14, 1970.
60. Ibid., January 18, 1970.
61. "Students and Soldiers Protest Closing of Antiwar Coffeehouse," *New York Times*, January 19, 1970, 4.
62. McAninch, "UFO," 4.
63. Giles, "Antiwar Movement in Columbia, South Carolina," 19.
64. USSF newsletter, January 24, 1970, http://sirnosir.com/archives_and_resources/library/pamphlets_publications.
65. *The State*, March 4, 1970.
66. Ibid., February 2, 1970, and February 5, 1970.
67. Giles, "Antiwar Movement in Columbia, South Carolina," 19.
68. Quoted in McAninch, "UFO," 7.
69. Myers, *Black, White, and Olive Drab*, 203.
70. Giles, "Antiwar Movement in Columbia, South Carolina," 19.
71. John D. Spade, "USC Group Says Foard 'Threatens Freedom,'" *The State*, May 1, 1970.
72. Ibid.
73. Quoted in McAninch, "UFO," 8.
74. For more on the John Foard saga, including details on his political connections and power over the university, see Lesesne, *History of the University of South Carolina*, 221–36.
75. Giles, "Antiwar Movement in Columbia, South Carolina," 26–29.
76. *Charlotte Observer*, June 8, 1970.
77. Myers, *Black, White, and Olive Drab*, 204.
78. Bass and Nelson, *Orangeburg Massacre*. On February 8, 1968, local police opened fire on a crowd of (largely black) students at the University of South Carolina, Orangeburg, just forty-five miles south of Columbia. The crowd was protesting the continued segregation at a local bowling alley. The incident preceded both the Jackson State and Kent State shootings later in the era and produced a flood of civil rights activism in the area. In Columbia, the UFO coffeehouse became a natural meeting place for activists in the wake of the Orangeburg shooting.

79. McAninch, "UFO."
80. Lesesne, *History of the University of South Carolina*, 235.
81. McAninch, "UFO," 7. McAninch details his discovery of Solicitor Foard's correspondences within a file that included the UFO trial transcript located at the Southern Regional Office of the ACLU in Atlanta, Georgia. The letters were sent to the office after Foard's death.

Chapter 4

1. Wills, *Nixon Agonistes*, 191. See also Perlstein, *Nixonland*, 657. According to Perlstein, by the time Nixon was elected, "Americans hated the war. They hated the antiwarriors more."
2. Cortright, *Soldiers in Revolt*, 13.
3. The most comprehensive institutional history of the U.S. military's transition to the all-volunteer force is Griffith, *U.S. Army's Transition to the All-Volunteer Force*. Other more sociologically driven histories include Rostker, *I Want You!*, and Flynn, *Draft*.
4. Appy, *Working Class War*, 51–60.
5. Foley, *Confronting the War Machine*. Foley's work separates the phenomenon of "draft-dodging" (evading the draft through fraudulent deferments, fleeing to Canada, or other means) from "draft resistance," which constituted young men taking political action against the draft, most often in the form of public protest and/or civil disobedience.
6. Cortright, *Soldiers in Revolt*, 84.
7. Vineberg and Taylor, *Summary and Review of Studies of the VOLAR Experiment, 1971*, 6.
8. "Hood Opens Coffee House," *Killeen Daily Herald*, October 28, 1971.
9. Fonda, *My Life So Far*, 238.
10. Lewis, *Hard Hats, Hippies, and Hawks*, 45.
11. *GI News and Discussion Bulletin*, no. 10, January 1972, 1.
12. Westmoreland's official title was Deputy Commander of Military Assistance Command, Vietnam, the military's generic name for all operations in Vietnam.
13. Steven V. Roberts, "Girls, Bands, and Ticker Tape Greet Troops from Vietnam in Seattle," *New York Times*, July 11, 1969.
14. "Royal Welcome Set for Vietnam Vets," *Tacoma News Tribune*, July 6, 1969, A2; "Cheers, Anti-war Chants Greet Returning Soldiers," *Seattle Times*, July 10, 1969, 1; "Token Pullout Met with Demand: Bring All the Troops Home Now!," *Militant*, July 25, 1969, 1; "Seattle Demonstrators: 'Bring 'em All Home!,'" *Militant*, July 25, 1969, 10.
15. Anderson, "GI Movement and the Response from the Brass," 98.
16. Cortright, *Soldiers in Revolt*, 55.
17. Daly, *Covering America*; Peck, *Uncovering the Sixties*; Starr, *Creation of the Media*. The rise of the underground press in the 1960s occurred within a longer historical period of corporate consolidation in the newspaper industry, which replaced the rich landscape of urban newspapers that had arisen in the nineteenth century with a relatively tiny group of elite media sources owned by multinational business interests. In New York City, for example, there were more than fifteen major news publications in circulation in 1900, yet by 1967 only three major newspapers (the *New York Times*, the *New York Post*, and the *New York Daily News*) remained. Though "counterculture" media's existence was

not entirely a reaction to this larger phenomenon, the increasingly closed-off nature of mainstream print journalism undoubtedly contributed to the popularity and appeal of alternative news sources in the 1960s and 1970s.

18. Memorandum, Major General Kenneth G. Wickham, Adjutant General, to Commanding Generals, May 28, 1969, subj.: Guidance on Dissent. National Archives and Records Administration, Record Group 472, box 14, 3.

19. Lewes, *Protest and Survive*, 83.

20. Quoted in Ostertag, *People's Movement, People's Press*, 141.

21. Quoted in ibid., 144.

22. Hajdu, *Ten-Cent Plague*; Duncan and Smith, *Power of Comics*, 53–54. Duncan and Smith credit *Mad* magazine as the inspiration for a whole generations of comic artists and publishers. By the early 1960s, they argue, *Mad*'s influence was evident not only in other comic publications but also in the wider aesthetic and attitude of American youth culture. This orientation made underground comics ("comix") inherently political: "Comix not only defied the sources of authority in conventional society by breaking their taboos, but they also went on the direct attack. Authority figures are presented as inept or brutish and always corrupt. The structures of society, institutions, and bureaucracies are portrayed as soulless and oppressive. As German media critics Rheinhold Reitberger and Wolfgang Fuchs correctly observed from their outside perspective, 'the underground cartoonists and their creations attack all that middle America holds dear.'" Duncan and Smith, *Power of Comics*, 53–54.

23. A series of books published by military leaders and critics in the 1970s took issue with the Vietnam-era Officer Corps and its focus on careerism and professionalization. See Gabriel and Savage, *Crisis in Command*; King, *Death of the Army*; and Grandstaff, "Making the Military American."

24. "The Hours of Boredom, the Seconds of Terror," *New York Times*, February 8, 1970.

25. Lifton, *Home from the War*, 231.

26. Barber, *Hard Rain Fell*, 15–19. For more on Black Power's impact on the New Left, see Joseph, *Waiting 'til the Midnight Hour*.

27. Quoted in Zinn, *Power of Nonviolence*, 39.

28. Quoted in Haas, *Assassination of Fred Hampton*, 27.

29. Halstead, *Out Now!*, 260–91. Halstead's internal history sheds light on the complicated racial dynamics within radical organizations of the late 1960s and early 1970s. For a military-specific perspective on race, see also Halstead, *GIs Speak Out against the War*; and Westheider, *Brothers in Arms*.

30. United States, Congress, House, Committee on Internal Security, *Investigation of Attempts to Subvert the United States Armed Services*, part 3, 7264–71.

31. *Marine Corps Gazette*, January 1971, 46.

32. *Black Unity*, vol. 1, no. 1, August 1970.

33. Zeiger, *History of the Oleo Strut Coffeehouse*, 22.

34. *GI News and Discussion Bulletin*, no. 10, January 1972, 61.

35. Ibid., 61.

36. Rossinow, "Revolution Is about Our Lives," 101–3. Substantial discussions of drugs and the antiwar movement can also be found in Gitlin, *Sixties*, 214–35; Miller, *Democracy Is in the Streets*, 278; and DeBenedetti and Chatfield, *American Ordeal*, 189.

37. Gould's monologue was featured in the Newsreel-produced film *Summer '68* (Norman Fruchter and John Douglas, 1969), which profiled the Oleo Strut along with a number of other New Left projects. Footage from *Summer '68* can also be seen in *Sir! No Sir!*

38. "GI Coffeehouse Opens," *Fun Travel Adventure*, no. 10, August 1969, Tamiment Library, New York University.

39. "Covered Wagon Rolls," *Helping Hand*, no. 10, September 1969.

40. "Haymarket Square," Project Report, *GI News and Discussion Bulletin*, no. 10, January 1972, 21. For more information on heroin abuse in the Vietnam-era U.S. military, see Westin and Shaffer, *Heroes and Heroin*.

41. "Fort Hood GI Haven," *Space City News*, Fall 1970.

42. Zeiger, *History of the Oleo Strut Coffeehouse*, 26.

43. Ibid., 25.

44. *GI News and Discussion Bulletin*, no. 10, January 1972, 23.

45. Ibid., 50.

46. Uhl, *Vietnam Awakening*, 52.

47. Yellin, *Our Mothers' War*, 86–88.

48. Faith, *Bob Hope*, xxii.

49. Alvin Shuster, "GIs in Vietnam High on Hope's Marijuana Jokes," *New York Times*, December 23, 1970.

50. "Bob Hope versus FTA," *Camp News*, vol. 3, no. 1, September 1971.

51. Howard Levy, interview by author, January 30, 2010. Levy confirmed many details of the FTA show's conception also found in Fred Gardner, "Hollywood Confidential, Part II," *Vietnam Generation Journal and Newsletter*, vol. 3, no. 3, November 1991. The FTA show is also discussed in Feiffer, *Backing into Forward*.

52. Though most GIs would recognize the acronym as meaning "Fuck the Army," the FTA show performers usually referred to the show's name (and overall message) as "Free the Army." The FTA show was also often referred to as the "USSF Show."

53. Gardner, "Hollywood Confidential, Part II."

54. Ibid.

55. The U.S. military's attempts at "repressive tolerance" throughout the Vietnam era are discussed in more detail in Bailey, *America's Army*.

56. Lacey Fosburgh, "Antiwar Troupe Formed to Tour Bases," *New York Times*, February 17, 1971.

57. "Left Face," *New Republic*, March 13, 1971, 9.

58. Michael Kernan, "GI Movement: A Show to Call Its Own," *Washington Post*, March 15, 1971.

59. James T. Wooten, "500 G.I.'s at Debut of Antiwar Show," *New York Times*, March 15, 1971.

60. "Antiwar Show for GIs Has Receptive Audience," *Camp News*, vol. 2, no. 2, March 1971.

61. Hershberger, *Jane Fonda's War*, 45; Roger Greenspun, "Jane Fonda's 'F.T.A.' Show Now a Film," *New York Times*, July 22, 1972.

62. "Antiwar Show for GIs Has Receptive Audience."

63. Fonda, *My Life So Far*, 273.

64. Quoted in Zeiger, *History of the Oleo Strut Coffeehouse*, 18.
65. "Fonda Brings Antiwar Show to Hood," *Killeen Daily Herald*, September 22, 1971.
66. Cortright, *Soldiers in Revolt*, 127–33.
67. Fonda, *My Life So Far*, 274.
68. Zeiger, *History of the Oleo Strut Coffeehouse*, 18.
69. Gardner, "Hollywood Confidential, Part II," 10.
70. Fred Gardner, "Case Study in Opportunism: The GI Movement," *Second Page Supplement*, October 1971, 7.
71. Hershberger, *Jane Fonda's War*, 46. The quote comes from Fonda's FBI file, LA 157-5089, 20. For more on the FTA show's impact on bases, see "Jane Fonda Antiwar Show Stage Near Fort Bragg," *New York Times*, March 14, 1973; Leticia Kent, "It's Not Just 'Fonda and Company,'" *New York Times*, March 21, 1971; "4,000 See 'Free the Army,'" *Honolulu Advertiser*, November 26, 1971; and Gary Arnold, "FTA: The Fonda Way," *Washington Post*, June 28, 1972.
72. "Strut Staff Raps," *Space City News*, October 1970.
73. Zeiger, *History of the Oleo Strut Coffeehouse*, 9.
74. Ibid., 10.
75. "Fort Hood GI Haven."
76. "The Oleo Strut," staff report, November 1, 1970, http://sirnosir.com/archives_and_resources/library/pamphlets_publications/oleo_strut/staff_report/page_1.html, accessed May 26, 2010. "ETS" stands for "Expiration of Term of Service." Since Fort Hood was one of the main return bases for soldiers back from Vietnam, many soldiers were discharged from the military and left Killeen, Texas, as a result. Some ETS's, as they were called, stayed in town, such as Dave Cline, who remained in Texas after his discharge to continue his activism against the war.
77. Ibid.
78. Zeiger, *History of the Oleo Strut Coffeehouse*, 10.
79. "Oleo Strut," staff report.
80. Zeiger, *History of the Oleo Strut Coffeehouse*, 11.
81. Ibid., 22.
82. Young, *Vietnam Wars*, 230–40.
83. Zeiger interview.
84. Activity at other western air force and navy bases included the creation of the Covered Wagon coffeehouse in Mountain Home, Idaho.
85. *Pacific Counseling Service* pamphlet, 1973, http://sirnosir.com/archives_and_resources/library/pamphlets_publications/repression/shelter_half/page1.html, accessed July 19, 2010.
86. Matthew Rinaldi, "The Olive-Drab Rebels: Military Organizing during the Vietnam Era," *Radical America* 8, May–June 1974, 45–46.
87. Jeffrey C. Alexander, "HPC Opening Its Offices to SDS Draft Counselors," *Harvard Crimson*, December 7, 1967.
88. Jones and Wessely, *Shell Shock to PTSD*.

89. "Pacific Counseling Center," box 3, folder 7, United States Servicemen's Fund Records, Wisconsin Historical Society. The PCS ultimately opened offices at U.S. military installations in Japan, Hawaii, the Philippines, and Korea.

90. Anderson, "GI Movement and the Response from the Brass," 110; "GIs for Peace Moves Ahead," *Camp News*, vol. 1, no. 7, January 15, 1971; "Farm Workers Press Lettuce Boycott," *Harvard Crimson*, November 13, 1970. Playing on young GIs' resentment of military authority, underground GI newspapers during this period frequently employed the slogan "Lifers Eat Lettuce."

91. *Strategies and Tactics for GI Organizing*, GI Alliance pamphlet, 1971, http://sirnosir.com/archives_and_resources/library/pamphlets_publications/repression/shelter_half/page1.html, accessed July 19, 2010.

92. "We Are One!," *Fed Up!*, vol. 2, no. 1, March 1971, Underground GI Newspapers, The Sixties Project digital archives.

93. "La Prensa Libre: Workers Strike Farah Co.," *Lewis-McChord Free Press*, July 1972, 7; "Cannery Workers," ibid., July 1972, 7. The University of Washington maintains an extensive website, "The Seattle Civil Rights and Labor History Project," at http://depts.washington.edu/civilr/, accessed June 19, 2011. The site contains numerous articles and primary sources that details the Pacific Northwest's history of radical labor and civil rights organizing.

94. Griffith, *U.S. Army's Transition to the All-Volunteer Force*, 190–93. Griffith's study describes how the army explicitly sought to expand the number of women in noncombat positions in the early 1970s, mainly as a way to fill personnel gaps in the absence of a draft system.

95. *Pacific Counseling Service* pamphlet.

96. Goldman, "Changing Role of Women in the Armed Forces," 892. See also Herbert, *Camouflage Isn't Only for Combat*.

97. *Pacific Counseling Service* pamphlet.

98. Griffith, *U.S. Army's Transition to the All-Volunteer Force*, 234. Griffith explains how military officials were worried that, in their rush to make military service more attractive to the general public, they had produced expectations about living and working conditions that the army was not prepared to meet. In a survey of sixty-four army generals in 1972, the army received reports of widespread unhappiness within the ranks and grouped the generals' suggestions into four major categories: "increased job satisfaction, better personnel management and leadership, improved living and working conditions, and improvement in the Army's public image." Ibid., 234.

99. Cortright, *Soldiers in Revolt*, 58. Chapter 4 provides more detail on the GI antiwar movement's shift in concentration to the navy and air force in the later years of the Vietnam War.

100. "Tenants Survey," *Lewis-McChord Free Press*, December 1971, 8; "Tenants Win Improvements," ibid., January 1972.

101. "The Good, the Bad, and the Ugly," ibid., February 1972, 7.

102. Lee, "Fed Up at Fort Lewis," 21–23.

103. *Fort Lewis Collective* pamphlet, 1974, http://sirnosir.com/archives_and_resources/library/pamphlets_publications/repression/shelter_half/page1.html, accessed July 19, 2010.

Epilogue

1. Jon R. Anderson, "New Era for Coffeehouses Rooted in Anti-war Tradition," *Army Times*, March 7, 2010.

2. The Central Committee for Conscientious Objectors was itself formed in 1948 in association with the return of the peacetime draft. The organization is dedicated to helping people avoid or resist military enlistment and was particularly active during the Vietnam War era.

3. Tod Ensign, "Shooting Pool Alone at Ft. Drum: Lessons for the GI Movement," *Veterans for Peace Newsletter*, July 2009.

4. Ibid.

5. Mark Thompson, "A Mounting Suicide Rate Prompts an Army Response," *Time*, December 14, 2009. For a comprehensive view of the PTSD crisis and related phenomena, see Finley, *Fields of Combat*.

Bibliography

ARCHIVAL COLLECTIONS

Contemporary Culture Collection, Temple University, Philadelphia, Pa.
   Underground GI Newspapers Collection
      Graffiti
      RITA-ACT
      Short Times
      Up against the Wall
National Archives and Records Administration, College Park, Md.
   Records of the Historical Services Division relating to army organizations and operations (1965–74)
   William Westmoreland Papers
Suzzallo Library, Special Collections, University of Washington, Seattle
Swarthmore College Peace Collection, Swarthmore, Pa.
   David Cortright Papers
   Underground GI Newspapers Collection
      Aboveground
      Bacon
      Dull Brass
      Fatigue Press
      Getting Together
      Gigline
      G.I. Voice
      Hair
      Head-On!
      Kill for Peace

       Left Face
       Liberated Barracks
       Marine Blues
       Military Law Project News-Notes
       Navy Times Are Changin'
       New Testament
       Next Step
       Omega
       Open Ranks
       Potemkin
       Semper Fi
       Up from the Bottom
       Veterans Stars and Strips for Peace
       Wildcat
       Your Military Left
    GI Movement Archive
Tamiment Library, New York University, New York
    Ally
    Anchorage Troop
    Committee for G.I. Rights Defense Committee
    Fort Hood 3 Defense Committee
    Fun Travel Adventure
    Great Lakes Movement for a Democratic Military
    National Mobilization Committee to End the War
    Off the Brass
    Servicemen's LINK to Peace
    U.S. Servicemen's Fund
    Vietnam Moratorium Committee (U.S.)
U.S. Army Heritage and Education Center, Carlisle Barracks, Pa.
    Individual Post Histories
        Fort Hood
        Fort Jackson
        Fort Lewis
Vietnam GI (personal collection)
Wisconsin Historical Society, Madison
    A Four Year Bummer
    Camp News
    Coffee House News
    GIs United against the War in Vietnam Correspondence
    Student Mobilization Committee to End the War in Vietnam Records
    United States Servicemen's Fund Records
    Up against the Bulkhead

Bibliography

DIGITAL ARCHIVES

Pacific Northwest Antiwar and Radical History Project, University of Washington, Seattle

Sir! No Sir! Dir. David Zeiger. Displaced Films, 2005. GI Movement Archives, Intertwingle New Media

The Sixties Project, Institute for Advanced Technology in the Humanities, University of Virginia

  Underground GI Newspapers

    About Face! The U.S Servicemen's Fund Newsletter
    As You Were
    Bond
    Counterpoint
    Duck Power
    Fed Up!
    Fun Travel Adventure
    GI C.L.D.C. Newsletter
    GI News and Discussion Bulletin
    G.I. Press Service
    Helping Hand
    Last Harass
    New SOS News
    Second Page Supplement
    Shakedown
    Vietnam Generation Journal and Newsletter
    WIN

Vietnam Center and Archive, Oral History Project, Texas Tech University, Lubbock

INTERVIEWS

All interview recordings are in the author's possession.
Coontz, Stephanie. Telephone interview by author. May 25, 2011.
Gardner, Fred. Interview by author. Alameda, Calif., January 15, 2011.
Garson, Barbara. Interview by author. New York, N.Y., May 7, 2011.
Gould, Josh. Telephone interview by author. January 25, 2010.
Levy, Howard. Interview by author. Brooklyn, N.Y., January 30, 2010.
Zeiger, David. Interview by author. Los Angeles, Calif., January 5, 2010.

REPORTS AND INVESTIGATIONS

Olson, Howard C., and R. William Rae. *Determination of the Potential for Dissidence in the US Army*. McLean, Va.: Research Analysis Corp., 1971.

United States. Congress. House. Committee on Internal Security. *Investigation of Attempts to Subvert the United States Armed Services, Parts 1–3: Hearings, Ninety-Second Congress, First Session*. Washington, D.C.: GPO, 1972.

———. *Subversive Involvement in Disruption of 1968 Democratic Party National Convention, Parts 1 and 2: Hearings before the Committee on Un-American Activities, House of Representatives, Ninetieth Congress, Second Session.* Washington, D.C.: GPO, 1968.

———. *The Workers World Party and Its Front Organizations.* Washington: United States Congress, 1974.

United States. Congressional Black Caucus Report. *Congressional Record.* 92nd Congress, 2nd Session. Washington, D.C., October 14, 1972.

U.S. District Court for the District of South Carolina (Columbia Division). *The U.F.O., Inc., et al. v. E. Harry Agnew.* Trial Transcript, April 25, 1970.

Vineberg, Robert, and Elaine N. Taylor. *Summary and Review of Studies of the VOLAR Experiment, 1971: Installation Reports for Forts Benning, Bragg, Carson, and Ord.* Alexandria, Va.: Human Resources Research Organization, 1972.

Westinghouse Electric Corporation, Center for Advanced Studies and Analyses. "Potential Impact of Cultural Change on the Navy in the 1970s." August 1, 1972.

NEWSPAPERS AND PERIODICALS

Black Panther
Columbia State
Commonweal
Ebony
Esquire
Fayetteville Observer
Guardian
Harper's
Journal of American History
Journal of Military History
Killeen (Tex.) Daily Herald
Liberation News Service
Life
Look
Los Angeles Times
Militant
Newsweek
New York Post
New York Times
New York Times Magazine
San Francisco Chronicle
Seattle Times
The State (Columbia, S.C.)
Tacoma News Tribune
Time
Wall Street Journal
Washington Post

DISSERTATIONS, THESES, AND PAPERS

Giles, Doris B. "The Antiwar Movement in Columbia, South Carolina 1965–1972." Seminar paper, South Caroliniana Library, University of South Carolina, Columbia, 1987.

Haines, Harry William. "The GI Underground Press: Two Case Studies of Alternative Military Newspapers." Master's thesis, University of Utah, 1976.

Hayes, James Robert. "The War within a War: Dissent in the Military with an Emphasis upon the Vietnam-Era." Ph.D. diss., University of Connecticut, 1975.

Hensley, William Edward. "The Vietnam Anti-war Movement: History and Criticism." Ph.D. diss., University of Oregon, 1979.

Keeney, Craig Mury. "Resistance: A History of Anti–Vietnam War Protests in Two Southern Universities, 1966–1970." Master's thesis, University of South Carolina, Columbia, 2003.

Kindig, Jessie. "Demilitarized Zone: The GI Movement and the Reorganization of the Military at Fort Lewis during the Vietnam War." Master's thesis, University of Washington, Seattle, 2008.

Kramer, Michael Jacob. "The Civics of Rock: Sixties Countercultural Music and the Transformation of the Public Sphere." Ph.D. diss., University of North Carolina, Chapel Hill, 2006.

Lair, Meredith H. "Beauty, Bullets, and Ice Cream: Re-imagining Daily Life in the 'Nam." Ph.D. diss., Pennsylvania State University, 2004.

Lee, Sam J. "Fed Up at Fort Lewis: A Regional History of the GI Protest Movement against the War in Vietnam." Master's thesis, Washington State University, 1997.

Moser, Richard. "From Deference to Defiance: America, the Citizen-Soldier and theVietnam Era." Ph.D. diss., Rutgers University Press, 1996.

Nobile, Vincent. "Political Opposition in the Age of Mass Media: GIs and Veterans against the War in Vietnam" Ph.D. diss., University of California at Irvine, 1987.

Retzer, Joseph David. "War and Political Ideology: The Roots of Radicalism amongVietnam Veterans." Ph.D. diss., Yale University, 1976.

Saunders, Alice. "Vietnam Vets against the War: The People's House in Clarksville, Tennessee (1970–1972)." Research paper, Northeastern University, 2007.

Seidman, Derek W. "The Unquiet Americans: GI Dissent during the Vietnam War." Ph.D. diss., Brown University, 2010.

Stacewicz, Richard A. "Winter Soldiers: An Oral History of the Vietnam Veterans Against the War." Ph.D. diss., University of Illinois, Chicago, 1997.

SECONDARY SOURCES

Albert, Judith Clavir, and Stewart Edward Albert, eds. *The Sixties Papers: Documents of a Rebellious Decade.* New York: Praeger, 1987.

Allah, Wakeel. *In the Name of Allah: A History of Clarence 13X and the Five Percenters.* Atlanta: A-Team Publishing, 2007.

Anderson, Terry H. "The GI Movement and the Response from the Brass." In *Give Peace a Chance: Exploring the Vietnam Antiwar Movement,* edited by Melvin Small and William D. Hoover, 93–115. Syracuse: Syracuse University Press, 1992.

Appy, Christian. *Patriots: The Vietnam War Remembered from All Sides.* New York: Viking, 2003.

———. *Working Class War: American Combat Soldiers and Vietnam.* Chapel Hill: University of North Carolina Press, 1993.

Bailey, Beth. *America's Army: Making the All-Volunteer Force.* Cambridge: Belknap Press of Harvard University Press, 2009.

Barber, David. *A Hard Rain Fell: SDS and Why It Failed.* Jackson: University Press of Mississippi, 2008.

Barnes, Peter. *Pawns: The Plight of the Citizen-Soldier.* New York: Knopf, 1972.

Bass, Jack, and Jack Nelson. *The Orangeburg Massacre.* New York: World Publishing, 1970.

Bederman, Gail. *Manliness and Civilization: A Cultural History of Gender and Race in the United States, 1880–1917.* Chicago: University of Chicago Press, 1995.

Bell County Historical Commission. *Story of Bell County, Texas*. 2 vols. Austin: Eakin Press, 1988.
Boyle, Brenda. *Masculinity in Vietnam War Narratives: A Critical Study of Fiction, Films and Nonfiction Writings*. Jefferson, N.C.: McFarland, 2009.
Boyle, Richard. *The Flower of the Dragon: The Breakdown of the U.S. Army in Vietnam*. San Francisco: Ramparts Press, 1972.
Braunstein, Peter, and Michael William Doyle, eds. *Imagine Nation: The AmericanCounterculture of the 1960s and '70s*. New York: Routledge, 2002.
Buzzanco, Robert. *Masters of War: Military Dissent and Politics in the Vietnam Era*. Cambridge: Cambridge University Press, 1996.
Chambers, John Whiteclay, ed. *The Oxford Companion to American Military History*. Oxford: Oxford University Press, 2000.
Christgau, Robert. "Phil Ochs, 1940–1976." *Village Voice*, April 19, 1976.
Cincinnatus [Cecil B. Currey]. *Self-Destruction: The Disintegration and Decay of the United States Army during the Vietnam Era*. New York: W. W. Norton, 1981.
Cleaver, Thomas McKelvey. "The Oleo Strut Coffeehouse and the GI Antiwar Movement." *Rag Blog*, http://theragblog.blogspot.com/2008/07/under-hood-anti-war-gi-coffeehouse-in.html. Accessed July 22, 2008.
Cohen, Lizabeth. *A Consumers' Republic: The Politics of Mass Consumption in Postwar America*. New York: Knopf, 2003.
Conroy, David. *In Public Houses: Drink and the Revolution of Authority in ColonialMassachusetts*. Chapel Hill: University of North Carolina Press, 1995.
Coppedge, Clay. "Ode to the Oleo Strut." *Texas Escapes Online Magazine*, http://www.texasescapes.com/ClayCoppedge/Ode-to-the-Oleo-Strut.htm. Accessed September 3, 2007.
Cortright, David. *Soldiers in Revolt: GI Resistance during the Vietnam War*. Chicago: Haymarket Books, 2005.
Cunningham, David. *There's Something Happening Here: The New Left, the Klan, and FBI Counterintelligence*. Berkeley: University of California Press, 2005.
Daly, Christopher. *Covering America: A Narrative History of a Nation's Journalism*. Amherst: University of Massachusetts Press, 2012.
Dane, Barbara. "The Oleo Strut." *Guardian*, July 30, 1968.
Davis, James Kirkpatrick. *Assault on the Left: The FBI and the Sixties Antiwar Movement*. Westport, Conn.: Praeger, 1997.
DeBenedetti, Charles, and Charles Chatfield. *An American Ordeal: The Antiwar Movement of the Vietnam Era*. Syracuse: Syracuse University Press, 1990.
DePastino, Todd. *Willie & Joe: The WW II Years—Bill Mauldin, Vols. 1 and 2*. Seattle: Fantagraphics Books, 2008.
Dickerson, James. *North to Canada: Men and Women against the Vietnam War*. Westport, Conn.: Praeger, 1999.
Duncan, Gra'Delle. *Killeen: A Tale of Two Cities*. Austin: Eakin Press, 1984.
Duncan, Randy, and Matthew J. Smith. *The Power of Comics: History, Form, and Culture*. New York: Continuum, 2009.
Engelhardt, Tom. *The End of Victory Culture: Cold War America and the Disillusioning of a Generation*. New York: Basic Books, 1995.

Enke, Anne. *Finding the Movement: Sexuality, Contested Space, and Feminist Activism.* Durham: Duke University Press, 2007.
Faith, William Robert. *Bob Hope: A Life in Comedy.* Cambridge, Mass.: Da Capo Press, 2003.
Farber, David. *Chicago '68.* Chicago: University of Chicago Press, 1994.
Feiffer, Jules. *Backing into Forward: A Memoir.* New York: Doubleday, 2010.
Fergus, Devin. *Liberalism, Black Power, and the Making of American Politics, 1965–1980.* Athens: University of Georgia Press, 2009.
Finley, Erin P. *Fields of Combat: Understanding PTSD among Veterans of Iraq andAfghanistan.* Ithaca: Cornell University Press (ILR), 2011.
Flynn, George Q. *The Draft: 1940–1973,* Lawrence: University Press of Kansas, 1993.
Foley, Michael S. *Confronting the War Machine: Draft Resistance during the Vietnam War.* Chapel Hill: University of North Carolina Press, 2003.
Fonda, Jane. *My Life So Far.* New York: Random House, 2005.
Frank, Thomas. *The Conquest of Cool: Business Culture, Counterculture, and the Rise of Hip Consumerism.* Chicago: University of Chicago Press, 1997.
Franklin, H. Bruce. *Vietnam and Other American Fantasies.* Amherst: University of Massachusetts Press, 2000.
Gabriel, Richard A., and Paul L. Savage. *Crisis in Command: Mismanagement in the Army.* New York: Hill and Wang, 1978.
Gallacci, Caroline, and Ron Karabaich. *Tacoma's Waterfront.* Charleston, S.C.: Arcadia, 2006.
Gardner, Fred. *The Unlawful Concert: An Account of the Presidio Mutiny Case.* New York: Viking Press, 1970.
Garfinkle, Adam M. *Telltale Hearts: The Origins and Impact of the Vietnam Antiwar Movement.* New York: St. Martin's Press, 1995.
Garrett, Banning, and Katherine Barkley, eds. *Two, Three . . . Many Vietnams: A Radical Reader on the Wars in Southeast Asia and the Conflicts at Home.* San Francisco: Canfield Press, 1971.
Gitlin, Todd. *The Sixties: Years of Hope, Days of Rage.* New York: Bantam Books, 1987.
Goldman, Nancy. "The Changing Role of Women in the Armed Forces." *American Journal of Sociology* 78, no. 4 (January 1973): 892–911.
Goodman, Mitchell. *The Movement toward a New America: The Beginning of a Long Revolution.* Philadelphia: Pilgrim Press, 1970.
Grandstaff, Mark R. "Making the Military American: Advertising, Reform, and the Demise of an Antistanding Military Tradition, 1945–1955." *Journal of Military History* 60, no. 2 (April 1996): 299–323.
Griffith, Robert K. *The U.S. Army's Transition to the All-Volunteer Force, 1968–1974.* Washington, D.C.: Center of Military History, U.S. Army, 1997.
Grose, Andrew. "Voices of Southern Protest during the Vietnam War Era." *Peace & Change* 32, no. 2 (April 2007): 153–67.
Haas, Jeffrey. *The Assassination of Fred Hampton: How the FBI and the Chicago PoliceMurdered a Black Panther.* Chicago: Chicago Review Press, 2009.
Hajdu, David. *The Ten-Cent Plague: The Great Comic Book Scare and How It Changed America.* New York: Farrar, Straus and Giroux, 2008.

Halstead, Fred. *GIs Speak Out against the War: The Case of the Ft. Jackson 8*. New York: Pathfinder Press, 1970.

———. *Out Now! A Participant's Account of the American Movement against the Vietnam War*. New York: Monad Press, 1978.

Heath, G. Louis, ed. *Mutiny Does Not Happen Lightly: The Literature of American Resistance to the Vietnam War*. Metuchen, N.J.: Scarecrow Press, 1976.

Heinl, Robert D., Jr. "The Collapse of the Armed Forces." *Armed Forces Journal* 108 (June 7, 1971): 30–38.

———. "Draftees vs. Lifers: Loser Is Army Morale." *Armed Forces Journal* 108 (May 3, 1971): 19.

Helmer, John. *Bringing the War Home: The American Soldier in Vietnam and After*. New York: Macmillan, 1974.

Herbert, Melissa S. *Camouflage Isn't Only for Combat: Gender, Sexuality, and Women in the Military*. New York: New York University Press, 1998.

Hershberger, Mary. *Jane Fonda's War: A Political Biography of an Antiwar Icon*. New York: New Press, 2005.

Hoffman, Abbie. *Soon to Be a Major Motion Picture*. New York: Putnam, 1980.

Hunt, Andrew E. *David Dellinger: The Life and Times of a Nonviolent Revolutionary*. New York: New York University Press, 2006.

———. *The Turning: A History of Vietnam Veterans Against the War*. New York: New York University Press, 1999.

Isserman, Maurice. *If I Had a Hammer: The Death of the Old Left and the Birth of the New Left*. New York: Basic Books, 1987.

Jeffreys-Jones, Rhodri. *The FBI: A History*. New Haven: Yale University Press, 2008.

Jones, Edgar, and Simon Wessely. *Shell Shock to PTSD: Military Psychiatry from 1900 to the Gulf War*. New York: Psychology Press, 2005.

Joseph, Peniel. *Waiting 'til the Midnight Hour: A Narrative History of Black Power in America*. New York: Henry Holt, 2006.

King, Edward. *The Death of the Army: A Pre-mortem*. New York: Saturday Review Press: 1972.

Learner, Laurence. *Paper Revolutionaries: The Rise of the Underground Press*. New York: Simon and Schuster, 1972.

Lembke, Jerry. *The Spitting Image: Myth, Memory, and the Legacy of Vietnam*. New York: New York University Press, 1998.

Lesesne, Henry H. *A History of the University of South Carolina, 1940–2000*. Columbia: University of South Carolina Press, 2001.

Lewes, James. *Protest and Survive: Underground GI Newspapers during the Vietnam War*. Westport, Conn.: Praeger, 2003.

Lewis, Penny. *Hard Hats, Hippies, and Hawks: The Vietnam Antiwar Movement as Myth and Memory*. Ithaca: Cornell University Press, 2013.

Lifton, Robert Jay. *Home from the War: Vietnam Veterans; Neither Victims nor Executioners*. New York: Basic Books, 1973.

Lutz, Catherine. *Homefront: A Military City and the American Twentieth Century*. Boston: Beacon Press, 2001.

Lynd, Alice, ed. *We Won't Go: Personal Accounts of War Objectors*. Boston: Beacon Press, 1968.
Mailer, Norman. *Armies of the Night: History as a Novel, the Novel as History*. New York: New American Library, 1968.
McAninch, William Shepard. "The UFO." *South Carolina Law Review* (Winter 1995): 363–79.
McCallum, Chris. *Yes to the Troops, No to the Wars: Quaker House, 40 Years of Front-line Peace Witness*. Catawissa, Pa.: Quaker House Books, 2009.
Miller, James. *Democracy Is in the Streets: From Port Huron to the Siege of Chicago*. New York: Simon and Schuster, 1987.
Moore, John Hammond. *Columbia and Richland County: A South Carolina Community, 1740–1990*. Columbia: University of South Carolina Press, 1993.
Moser, Richard. *The New Winter Soldiers: GI and Veteran Dissent during the Vietnam Era*. New Brunswick, N.J.: Rutgers University Press, 1996.
Myers, Andrew H. *Black, White, and Olive Drab: Racial Integration at Fort Jackson, South Carolina*. Charlottesville: University of Virginia Press, 2006.
Navasky, Victor S. *Naming Names*. New York: Hill and Wang, 2003.
Nicosia, Gerald. *Home to War: A History of the Vietnam Veterans' Movement*. New York: Three Rivers Press, 2001.
Oldenburg, Ray. *The Great Good Place: Cafés, Coffee Shops, Community Centers, Beauty Parlors, General Stores, Bars, Hangouts, and How They Get You through the Day*. New York: Paragon House, 1989.
Oppenheimer, Martin, ed. *The American Military*. New Brunswick, N.J.: Transaction, 1971.
Ostertag, Bob. *People's Movements, People's Press: The Journalism of Social Justice Movements*. Boston: Beacon Press, 2006.
Pattison, Robert. *The Triumph of Vulgarity: Rock Music in the Mirror of Romanticism*. New York: Oxford University Press, 1987.
Peck, Abe. *Uncovering the Sixties: The Life and Times of the Underground Press*. New York: Pantheon Books, 1985.
Pendergrast, Mark. *Uncommon Grounds: The History of Coffee and How It Changed Our World*. New York: Basic Books, 1999.
Perlstein, Rick. *Nixonland: The Rise of a President and the Fracturing of America*. New York: Scribner, 2008.
Putnam, Robert. *Bowling Alone: The Collapse and Revival of American Community*. New York: Simon and Schuster, 2001.
Rinaldi, Matthew. "The Olive-Drab Rebels: Military Organizing during the Vietnam Era," *Radical America* 8 (May–June 1974).
Rossinow, Doug. "The Revolution Is about Our Lives: The New Left's Counterculture." In *Imagine Nation: The American Counterculture of the 1960s and '70s*, edited by Peter Braunstein and Michael William Doyle, 99–104. New York: Routledge, 2002.
Rostker, Bernard. *I Want You! The Evolution of the All-Volunteer Force*. Santa Monica, Calif.: RAND Corporation, 2006.
Rowe, John Carlos, and Rick Berg, eds. *The Vietnam War and American Culture*. New York: Columbia University Press, 1991.

Sale, Kirkpatrick. *SDS*. New York: Vintage Books, 1974.
Sayre, Nora. *Sixties Going on Seventies: Revised Edition*. New Brunswick, N.J.: Rutgers University Press, 1996.
Sayres, Sohnya, et al., eds. *The 60s without Apology*. Minneapolis: University of Minnesota Press, 1984.
Schulman, Bruce J. *From Cotton Belt to Sunbelt: Federal Policy, Economic Development, and the Transformation of the South, 1938–1980*. Durham: Duke University Press, 1994.
———. *The Seventies: The Great Shift in American Culture, Society, and Politics*. Cambridge, Mass.: Da Capo Press, 2001.
Schulzinger, Robert D. *A Companion to American Foreign Relations*. Oxford: Blackwell Publishing, 2003.
Shafer, D. Michael. *The Legacy: The Vietnam War in the American Imagination*. Boston: Beacon Press, 1990.
Sherrill, Robert. *Military Justice Is to Justice as Military Music Is to Music*. New York: Harper and Row, 1970.
Small, Melvin. *Antiwarriors: The Vietnam War and the Battle for America's Hearts and Minds*. Wilmington, Del.: SR Books, 2002.
Small, Melvin, and William D Hoover, eds. *Give Peace a Chance: Exploring the Vietnam Antiwar Movement*. Syracuse: Syracuse University Press, 1992.
Smith, Emily Farrington. *Fayetteville, North Carolina: An All-American History*. Charleston, S.C.: History Press, 2011.
Sorkin, Michael. *Variations on a Theme Park: The New American City and the End of Public Space*. New York: Macmillan, 1992.
Sossi, Ron, ed. *Voices of the Chicago Eight: A Generation on Trial*. San Francisco: City Lights Books, 2008.
Stacewicz, Richard. *Winter Soldiers: An Oral History of the Vietnam Veterans Against the War*. New York: Twayne, 1997.
Staples, William G. *The Encyclopedia of Privacy*. Westport, Conn.: Greenwood Press, 2007.
Stapp, Andy. *Up against the Brass*. New York: Simon and Schuster, 1970.
Starr, Paul. *The Creation of the Media: Political Origins of Mass Communication*. New York: Basic Books, 2005.
Swarner, Ken. *The Evergreen Post: A History of Fort Lewis*. Tacoma, Wash.: Ranger Publishing, 1993.
Terry, Wallace, ed. *Bloods: An Oral History of the Vietnam War*. New York: Random House, 1984.
Uhl, Michael. *Vietnam Awakening: My Journey from Combat to the Citizens' Commission of Inquiry on U.S. War Crimes in Vietnam*. Jefferson, N.C.: McFarland, 2007.
Wachsberger, Ken. *Voices from the Underground: Insider Histories of the Vietnam Era (Vols. 1 & 2)*. Tempe: Mica Press, 1993.
Waterhouse, Larry G., and Mariann G. Wizard. *Turning the Guns Around: Notes on the GI Movement*. New York: Praeger, 1971.
Wells, Tom. *The War Within: America's Battle over Vietnam*. Berkeley: University of California Press, 1994.

Westheider, James E. *Brothers in Arms: The African American Experience in Vietnam.* Lanham, Md.: Rowman and Littlefield, 2008.
Westin, Av, and Stephanie Shaffer. *Heroes and Heroin: The Shocking Story of Drug Addiction in the Military.* New York: Pocket Books, 1972.
Wills, Garry. *Nixon Agonistes: The Crisis of the Self-Made Man.* New York: Houghton Mifflin, 1969.
Wolfe, Tom. *The Electric Kool-Aid Acid Test.* New York: Bantam Books, 1969.
Yellin, Emily. *Our Mothers' War: American Women at Home and at the Front during World War II.* New York: Simon and Schuster, 2005.
Young, Marilyn. *The Vietnam Wars: 1945–1990.* New York: HarperCollins, 1991.
Zeiger, David. "Did the GI Movement End the Vietnam War? And What Is the Real Legacy of the GI Coffeehouses?" Different Drummer Cafe, http://www.differentdrummercafe.org/gi movement.html. Accessed April 19, 2010.
———. *History of the Oleo Strut Coffeehouse, 1968–1972.* Sir! No Sir! Digital Archive, http://sirnosir.com/archives_and_resources/library/pamphlets_publications. Accessed July 19, 2010.
Zinn, Howard. *A People's History of the United States: 1492–Present.* New York: HarperCollins, 1980.
———. *The Power of Nonviolence: Writings by Advocates of Peace.* Boston: Beacon Press, 2002.

Index

Agnew, Harry T., 82, 84
Ali, Muhammad, 36, 97
All-volunteer force, 10, 89, 115–19, 137 (n. 3)
American Servicemen's Union (ASU), 6, 60, 64, 132 (n. 72)
Anderson, Stan, 38–40
"Aquatic Invasion of Fort Lewis," 8, 61–63
Armed Farces Days, 52–57, 114, 131 (n. 44)

Beatles, The, 20, 67
Black Power, 11, 96–99, 138 (n. 26)
Blumsack, Martin, 23

Carmichael, Stokely, 96
Carson, Wade, 78
Chase, Richard, 8, 44–48
Chavez, Cesar, 116
Chomsky, Noam, 25, 134 (n. 24)
Cline, Dave, 49, 52–56, 94, 140 (n. 76)
Cohen, Leonard (activist), 82, 84
Columbia, S.C., 4, 7; city history, 18–22; UFO coffeehouse in, 24–28, 36, 41–42, 70, 75; coffeehouse trial in, 79–87, 121
Committee on Internal Security, 68, 86, 134 (n. 9)

Coontz, Stephanie, ix, 61–63, 133 (n. 81)
Covered Wagon (coffeehouse), 8, 73–74, 101, 109–10
Cunningham, Cam, 56, 132 (n. 59)

Davis, Rennie, 8, 24–25, 66–67
Dellums, Ron (U.S. representative), 58
Democratic National Convention (Chicago 1968), 4, 44–46, 66
Deutsch, Daniel, 72
Different Drummer Café, 123–24
Drugs, 17, 21–22, 75, 82–86, 100–103
Duncan, Donald, 3

Fayetteville, N.C., 5, 9, 92–94, 101, 106–9,
Ferré, Merle, and Robert Duane, 81–84
Foard, John (5th Circuit solicitor), 83–86, 137 (n. 81)
Fonda, Jane, 10; and Oleo Strut coffeehouse, 51–52, 90; and FTA show, 105–13
Fort Bragg Women's Project, 5
Fort Dix Coffeehouse, 5, 74
Fort Hood 43, 4, 44–45
Fort Hood Three, 2–3

Fort Hood United Front, 57–59, 98–99, 114
Fort Jackson: institutional history of, 18–23; and GI movement, 36–44, 60, 79–87
Fort Jackson Eight, 8, 36–44, 79–87
Fort Knox Coffeehouse, 8, 70–74, 101
Fort Lewis, 7–8; institutional history of, 33–36; and GI movement, 37–39, 61–64, 76–78, 115–19
FTA ("Free the Army" or "Fuck the Army"), 10, 70, 106
FTA show, 10, 103–11, 140 (n. 71)

Gardner, Fred, ix, 3–4, 7, 15–41, 51, 86, 103–6, 110, 120–24
Garson, Barbara, 38–39, 106
GI-Civilian Alliance for Peace (GI-CAP), 60–61
GI Rights Network, 122
GIs United Against the War in Vietnam, 42, 86
Gould, Josh, 28, 30, 45–46, 100, 111
Gregory, Dick, 107–8, 134 (n. 24)

Harvard Crimson, 15
Harvey, Kelvin, 57, 114
Hayden, Tom, 8, 24, 66–67
Haymarket Square Coffeehouse, 5, 101–3, 107–8
Heinl, Colonel Robert L., 67–68, 133 (n. 7), 134 (n. 12)
Hew-Kekaw-Na-Yo (GI organization), 79
Hoover, J. Edgar, 75
Hope, Bob, 104–5, 108
House Un-American Activities Committee (HUAC), 66–67, 134 (nn. 9, 13)

Ichord, Richard (U.S. representative), 68

Kent State shootings, 53, 85, 136 (n. 78)
King, Martin Luther, Jr., 44, 97

Killeen, Texas, 7–8, 28–36, 44–46, 50–60, 70–73, 90–92, 100–104, 109–14, 121
Kraus, Jon, 82, 85

Leesville, LA, 16–17, 28
Leon, Reverend Gonzalo, 82
Lettuce boycott, 116–17, 141 (n. 90)
Levy, Howard, 3, 15; and USSF, 25–27, 43, 74–75, 83; and FTA show, 104–6, 126 (n. 9)
Lifton, Robert Jay, 96
Lockard, Jay, 28–30, 111

Mailer, Norman, 24, 80, 127 (n. 33)
McChord Air Force Base, 33–34, 117–21
McLellan, D. H., 39
McNair, Robert (governor), 85
Mickleson, Donna, 20, 121
Miles, Joe, 42–44
Morrow, Rowland A., 69
Mountain Home, Idaho, 8, 73–74, 101, 109
Movement for a Democratic Military (MDM), 74, 97–98
Muldraugh, Kentucky, 8, 70–71, 101
Myerson, Alan, 20

National Mobilization Committee to End the War in Vietnam (Mobe); and Summer of Support, 24–25; and Democratic National Convention, 65–66
Nixon, Richard, 9, 34, 53, 62, 67, 76, 85, 88–92, 114

Oleo Strut coffeehouse, 7–8, 28–33, 44–60, 70–73, 90, 94, 98–104, 109–45
Operation Garden Plot, 47–48, 95

Pacific Counseling Service (PCS), 116–18, 141 (n. 89)
People's Justice Committee, 59, 99, 114
Peterson, Bruce, 32–33
Petrick, Howard, 60

Index

Post-traumatic stress disorder, 11, 116
Priest, John, 57, 114

Quaker House, 9

Rinaldi, Matthew, 76
Rivers, L. Mendel, 22

Seattle, Washington, 33–36, 60–63, 77, 92, 115–18
Shelter Half (coffeehouse), 7–8, 36–40, 60–64, 76–79, 114–20
Socialist Workers Party, 6, 35–36, 43, 60–61. *See also* Young Socialist Alliance
Spock, Benjamin, 25
Spring Offensive Committee (GI-SOC), 54–55
Stapp, Andy, 6, 60, 64, 132 (n. 72)
Stauffacher, H. W., 64
Stokes, Louis (U.S. representative), 58–59, 132 (n. 68)
Students for a Democratic Society (SDS), 1, 6, 28, 35, 61, 96–97, 115
Summer of Support, 4, 7, 23–24, 36, 40
Sutherland, Donald, 10, 105, 107–109

Tacoma, Washington, 7–8; city history, 33–40; and GI movement, 60–63, 76–77, 92, 114–19
Thurmond, Strom, 22
Tyrrell's Jewelry, 8, 55–57, 132 (nn. 59, 61)

UFO (coffeehouse), 4, 7–8; and Columbia, S.C., 20–25, 28; and Fort Jackson Eight case, 41–44, 70; on trial, 79–87, 121
Under the Hood Café, 121
Uniform Code of Military Justice (UCMJ), 26, 93, 98, 127 (n. 42)
United Farm Workers, 79, 132 (n. 60)
United States Servicemen's Fund (USSF), 25–28, 33, 70, 73–75, 94, 100–113
University of South Carolina, 82–84
University of Washington, 35–36, 61, 77, 141 (n. 93)

Vietnam Veterans Against the War, 17, 24
Volunteer Army (VOLAR), 10, 89–90, 115–18

Westmoreland, William, 92
Williams, Wes, 58–59, 114
Williams Bay, Wisconsin, 10, 91, 99
Wrightstown, New Jersey, 74

Young Socialist Alliance (YSA), 6, 35–36, 42, 61, 128 (n. 73). *See also* Socialist Workers Party

Zabriskie Point (film), 51
Zeiger, David, ix, 54–55, 102, 110–14